The Rent Control Debate

Urban and Regional Policy and Development Studies

Michael A. Stegman, General Editor

The Rent Control Debate

Edited by Paul L. Niebanck

The University of North Carolina Press
Chapel Hill and London

© 1985 The University of North Carolina Press
All rights reserved
Manufactured in the United States of America
Library of Congress Cataloging in Publication Data
Main entry under title:
The rent control debate.
(Urban and regional policy and development studies)
Includes index.
1. Rent Control—United States—Addresses, essays,
lectures. I. Niebanck, Paul L. II. Series.
HD7288.82.R46   1985   363.5'6'0973   85-1181
ISBN 0-8078-1670-1
ISBN 0-8078-4142-0 (pbk.)

Designed by Neil Morgan.
Set in 10/12 pt Times Roman.

Contents

Tables

Acknowledgments

As a collaborative effort, this book's strengths and weaknesses derive from both the capabilities of us as individual authors and the inevitable difficulties involved in negotiating the differences that exist between and among us. Of enormous importance in this regard was the opportunity we had at one point to come together, to share our work and to offer each other critical advice. The occasion was provided by the combined efforts of Robert L. Sinsheimer, chancellor of the University of California at Santa Cruz, and Peggy Musgrave, professor of Economics and director of the Seminar in Public Finance and Applied Economics at the same institution. Present at that meeting were a number of other colleagues, notably Michael Teitz, professor of City and Regional Planning at the University of California, Berkeley, who chaired our conversations; Michael K. Orbach, now associate professor of Anthropology at East Carolina University, who synthesized the responses of our larger audience; and Suzanne Holt, assistant professor of Economics at Santa Cruz. Professor Holt's participation was crucial. She conceived the event, selected the participants, and encouraged us to establish an agenda of thought that could result in a book of responsible coverage and depth. To each of these persons, and to Carol Fairhurst, of Quik-Key Quality Typing Service in Santa Cruz, who so ably typed the manuscript, we offer our thanks. The combined effort has been a satisfying and productive one. Our intention is that it will be a useful one as well.

Introduction

The literature on rent control is fragmentary, its data local. Although there has been a proliferation of local studies, no synthesis has emerged. The needs of professionals, scholars, and citizens with interest in the subject thus have not been fully met.

It is a time of important transition in the housing market and great uncertainty in the politics of housing. It is time to define the major issues related to rent control, provide guidelines to inform policy, and establish a foundation for more extensive and systematic study. Such are the purposes of this book.

Chapter 1 describes the conditions that have brought rent control to the surface of public consciousness, and it outlines the reservations and criticisms with which rent control initiatives typically are faced.

Chapter 2 broadens the framework, outlines the relevant features of the fast-changing national housing system, and directly links rent control with the services that the rental sector will be called upon to render in the years just ahead.

Chapters 3 and 4 form a pair. Together, they describe the rent control reality in considerable and balanced detail. The former provides an overview of the New York City law as it has evolved since World War II and probes the effects of that law through time. The latter analyzes rent control in California. Contrary to New York, where the experience is lengthy and geographically limited, California's rent control is of recent origin, is scattered throughout the state, and is extremely diverse in its characteristics.

Chapters 5 and 6 constitute another pair; they bring a methodological perspective to the substantive issue. The former provides an example of what it takes to isolate the market variables that are associated with rent control. The analysis, based on a linear multiple regression model, questions certain aspects of the conventional wisdom regarding housing systems. In contrast to Chapter 5, Chapter 6 deals with effects rather than causes and focuses on intra-city rather than inter-city phenomena. This chapter uses a simple difference equation to reveal the influence of rent control on the quality of the housing supply.

Chapter 7 concludes with a set of critical reflections on what seems to be known about rent control and what still needs to be known. It appeals for scholarly attention to the rent control phenomenon and the political economy that it seeks to influence. Surely a device with so much potential for use—and misuse—in the present era deserves to be understood with greater clarity and authority than has been possible thus far.

The Rent Control Debate

The Politics and Economics of Rent Control

by Paul L. Niebanck

America's housing dilemma has rekindled an interest in rent control as an instrument of policy at the local level.[1] Three communities where rent control has been recently debated give evidence of the vitality of the issue.

Pembroke Park, Florida, is a tiny incorporated town that lies between the burgeoning cities of Miami to the south and Fort Lauderdale to the north. Development pressures from both directions are immense, and the value of land for commercial or high-priced residential uses has skyrocketed. The town's population, representing barely one-fifth of 1 percent of the regional population, is predominantly older people, stable residents, singles, and couples. They live primarily in mobile homes, and typically they subsist on low and moderate fixed incomes.

These mobile home occupants want rent control, and at a public hearing in November 1983, attended by hundreds of affected persons, their testimony was unified and insistent. "We are captives." "There is nowhere to go." "Rents have risen ninety percent in five years." "I have forty dollars left for medical expenses." "Our bargaining position is unequal." "We can't trust the landlords."[2]

Recognizing the expensive—and possibly futile—legal battle that would ensue if rent control were enacted, the town commission rejected the pleas of its constituents that night in November. Advocates wasted no time, thereupon, in taking steps to recall the naysayers.

Fort Lee, New Jersey, located across the George Washington

Bridge from Manhattan Island, is a traditional middle-class suburb of homeowners. A rash of high-rise apartment construction occurred during the 1960s, and by the mid-1970s, a majority of the voters were occupants of the new rental stock. Their political power had become strong enough to pass a restrictive rent control law—one that would hold annual rents well below the then prevailing increases in the cost of living—and they did so.

Inflation, especially the escalation of energy costs, which were passed on to tenants, triggered the demand for rent control in Fort Lee, and affluent tenants (typically in the top twentieth income bracket, statewide) have been the beneficiaries of the law. Since the institution of controls, interest in rent control has subsequently become muted, but so has inflation. The law remains in force, a safeguard against renewed market pressures on the rents of luxury apartments.

Santa Cruz, California, is a moderate-sized coastal city, geographically independent and a hothouse for cultural and political innovation. Young people have migrated to the area; environmentalists have successfully introduced strict growth limitations at both county and city levels; housing scarcity has boosted prices; and rent levels have turned sharply upward. The market prices of ordinary rental accommodations seem, to many of their occupants, to bear no reasonable relationship to their real value as habitats. Perceived profit-taking is resented; interest in cooperative ownership is evident; and the whole issue has taken on explicit ideological dimensions.

Twice defeated in the late 1970s, rent control was introduced, again by initiative, in early 1982. Piggybacking a city council campaign that secured a first-time majority for self-described socialists and feminists, proponents of rent control put forward what would have been as stringent a law as exists in the state. The initiative overshot its mark, and was eventually defeated at the polls, but even its opponents have conceded the possibility that rent control may soon become the law in Santa Cruz.

A Response to Housing Deprivation

The above-mentioned localities where rent control has been advocated reveal a framework for understanding America's changing housing situation. Proponents of rent control have said, "A renter's revolt has swept across the nation. . . . It will rival the Civil Rights Movement of the 60's in both scope and intensity. The battle will be one of human rights versus property rights."[3] In Pembroke Park, Fort Lee, and Santa Cruz, people across a broad spectrum have shown their readiness to consider rent control seriously as a local policy. Their witness is that three principal features of the housing situation need to be improved.

1. *Shelter poverty.* The budgets of more and more American households simply cannot tolerate the high proportion of income that is required to pay for housing. Such households, if they are to live in decent housing at all, have no alternative but to sacrifice their food consumption, their health care, their education, and other necessities in order to do so.

In its present dimensions, shelter poverty is a recent phenomenon in American life. It affects more than ten million lower-income households, three-fourths of whom are renters.[4] To put the matter plainly: Even if low-income households could afford to pay as much as 25 percent of their incomes for housing, which they usually cannot, they would find that two such households would be competing for every unit available at that price.[5]

The term, "shelter poverty," could be said to be derived from the more homespun phrase, "house poor." The folk version of the term implies that a household (perhaps foolishly, perhaps wisely) has acquired more shelter space than it needs and that, because of its overconsumption, it is constrained from spending time, energy, or money on other pursuits. Shelter poverty, as we know it today, is not so benign. It is initiated and perpetuated not by individual choice, but by the increasingly unequal distribution of income and wealth in our society, and by the structure of jobs and other opportunities that sustains that inequality. It is exacerbated by the withdrawal of federal housing subsidies for poor people and by the factors that have led to the high costs of housing production. Its victims need relief through lower housing prices, among other avenues.

2. *Housing inflation.* In recent years, the inflation in housing prices has been quite extraordinary. The price of land, the price of the building, and the price of money have exceeded not only the rate of inflation experienced in other markets but also any increase in real income. This is primarily evident in the price of a standard new house produced for owner occupancy. Holding the basic features of a new house constant through time, its price rose by almost three and one-half times between the late 1960s and the early 1980s.[6] Further, changes in financing arrangements and interest rates have combined with the increase in price to exclude all but the most affluent quintile of the population from the possibility of ever purchasing a new home.

The price inflation of new housing for private ownership has reverberated throughout the housing stock. As housing standards have changed, as markets have interacted, and as demand groups have adapted, the rental inventory itself has come to reflect the price characteristics of the new ownership component. While inflation in the rental sector has tended historically to lag behind inflation in the ownership sector, this superficial fact may now be more an illusion than a reality. Standardized for what the consumer gets for his or her outlay, the net costs associated with renting may actually be equal to—or higher than—the costs of owning. And, housing inflation in the rental sector falls equally on both the rich and the poor.

3. *Alienation from "home."* Identifying with, taking responsibility for, and having control over one's abode is difficult in a society as mobile as ours. Among renters, the absence of a sense of belonging, and a consequent absence of stewardship for the housing unit, appear to be chronic conditions. The responses of landlords are often formal and minimal, and the rewards to the occupant of investing in upkeep and improvement are few and transitory. Rental occupancy is often reluctant; commitments are

meager; and one's sense of self-worth is diminished. The simple fact that the unit is not "ours," or that it is not owned or managed by a caring institution in which "we" have membership, discourages occupants from thinking of it as home.

Some observers would, in the face of what here is called alienation from home, seek a "decommodification" of housing. "Housing for people, not profits!" would be their rallying cry. In addition to traditional concerns for size, quality, and cost, they would emphasize qualities of identification and autonomy in defining what is good housing: "[The] primary goal [is] to provide every person with housing that is affordable, adequate in size and of decent quality, *secure in tenure, and located in a supportive neighborhood of choice, with recognition of the special housing problems confronting oppressed groups* (emphasis ours)."[7] Others have gone so far as to specify the preferred forms of tenure: "[P]rivate rental housing [must be] converted into forms of social ownership, such as non-equity or low-equity co-ops, life estate condominiums, ownership by community trusts, or public ownership."[8] These alternatives could reduce the costs of residency. And, to persons who are not able or anxious to own their housing in fee simple, these alternatives could also represent ways to restore a mutually enhancing relationship between housing units and householders. Such a restoration would be of immense value and is long overdue.

Perception and Deception

It is no coincidence that the local situations in which rent control is an active issue reveal the main contours of America's housing dilemma. Rent control is a device that is widely perceived to have the capacity to stave off the worst effects of shelter poverty, housing inflation, and alienation from home, and it is a device that can be employed directly by counties and cities, whatever the level of commitment may be in the private sector or at more remote levels of government.

Obvious as rent control might appear as a means to protect the renter population, however, such a conclusion must be accompanied by a sharp warning: In the long run, rent control may prove to have contributed to the very conditions that have quickened our interest in it. Whatever power it may have to inhibit a perceived evil, rent control—given its narrow, short-range, and essentially adversarial character—may not have the power to mitigate that evil.

Shelter poverty provides an example. Rent control does nothing to bring additional housing into the rental supply, but it can induce new demand for rental housing within affluent demand sectors in which the tenure decision is sensitive to price. In the face of supply limitations, these new demands must be satisfied in part through the preemption of relatively high quality existing units. Households whose demand position does not allow them to compete effectively must then accept units of lower quality. The operational result of such transfers is to increase the size of the shelter-impoverished population and to intensify the burden on its poorest members. It is arguable, therefore, that shelter poverty can actually become more severe under rent control.

Similarly, while rent control seems to address directly and decisively the specter of housing inflation, it may do so only by a limited and transitory definition. Insofar as its existence actively discourages moderately priced new construction and encourages withdrawals from the lower priced rental inventory, the aggregate result could be an upward shift in rents. Published rents for individual units might well be stabilized, but simultaneously the structure of rents could actually rise. A diminution of housing opportunity following the enactment of rent control ordinances could result in effective increases in rents at all levels of occupant income and housing quality.

The matter of alienation from home is a more subtle matter, but even here there is a negative potential. The less control the owner of rental housing has over price, the more control he or she may seek to have over the other attributes of the unit, including the owner-tenant relationship. Occupancy criteria may become more stringent, for instance, and whatever interest there previously might have been in negotiated improvements in quality could wane. More important, perhaps, owners under rent control may seek ways to escape their obligations altogether, and actual divestment may occur with increased frequency. In such instances, it is typical that the occupants who are the farthest removed from an active relationship with their housing unit are most likely to suffer. Rather than giving occupants more influence, rent control could prove to have deprived them of the modicum of stability and belonging that existed before control was instituted.

Such responses as the ones just described often seem hypothetical and unacceptable to persons in housing distress. But while they are not palpable, they are nonetheless quite real. And to the degree that they occur, they can undermine the well-being of just the kinds of persons whom rent control would seek to assist. By limiting the amounts that can be paid for rental housing, rent control may serve to limit the level of housing supply, reduce the quality and security of the opportunities that are available, and even increase the relative rent burden. What appears initially to be a control on the power of the housing supplier to establish the price of occupancy may prove at the extreme to be a control over the power of the demander—however meager—to secure desirable housing at any price.

Opponents of rent control have held that rent control discourages the construction of rental housing; that it leads to under-maintenance, abandonment, demolition, and conversion to more profitable use; and that it deprives tenants and prospective tenants by introducing discriminatory and illegal behaviors into the market transaction.[9] These arguments deserve respect. They are grounded in a knowledge of the incentives and expectations that govern the provision of rental housing in the United States, and they are testimony to the capacity of the housing market to swallow up or contradict the best intentions of rent control.

Thus, rent control has the quality of an enigma. It seems to be exactly the kind of response that the prevailing housing situation demands. Certainly it has its origins in the most troubling aspects of that situation. But its power as a regulatory device seems also to have a dark side. Simultaneously, rent control invites widespread use and seems to defy its own useful image.

Just as advocacy of rent control has increased, so has the resistance to its implementation. Largely in response to Pembroke Park's recent enthusiasm, lobbyists have hastened to secure a state law in Florida that would preempt the right of localities to establish rent control. Similar efforts have been made in California in reaction to pro-rent control efforts such as those in Santa Cruz. And where political avenues seem closed, myriad other ways can be found to deflate the rent control movement. Not the least of these is condominium conversion, which in Fort Lee has become extensive since the introduction of rent control. These reactions are evidence of both the political vitality of the issue and the important social and economic claims that are at stake. Further, they demonstrate that the market conditions within which rent control must realistically be evaluated are themselves often uncertain and unreliable.

The Market Structure of the Rental Sector

by George Sternlieb & James W. Hughes

Housing in the United States is in a period of rapid transition. Initially, after World War II, increases in the real purchasing power of America's citizenry supported a tidal wave of privately owned, single family housing. In more recent years it was sustained by the impetus of inflationary expectations. But the economy, with changes in financing, a decline in real purchasing power, and deflation, has fundamentally altered the housing market. The changes in the financial arena and the decline in real house buying power are both powerful forces, whose consequences are exaccr-bated by the potential for deflation.

This chapter presents a set of data against which alternative futures may be contrasted. The incongruity of historical events, in terms of the probability of their continuation and their value as guidance for the future, is analyzed in relation to rent control. While rent control is essentially a localized phenomenon, respond-ing to particular conditions, the local conditions themselves have become increasingly dependent on national market factors. As rent control becomes more widespread, moreover, it is probable that it will have an independent influence on these factors.

The Dynamics of the Last Two Decades

During the course of the past twenty years, the housing shortage in the United States that had resulted from the Great Depression and World War II was greatly diminished. For every two housing units that existed in 1960, there were three units in 1980 (Table 2.1).

Table 2.1

Changes in the United States Housing Inventory, 1960, 1970, and 1980 (Numbers in Thousands)

	1960	1970	1980
All housing units	58,326	68,672	88,397
Year-round units	56,584	67,699	86,678
Occupied units	53,024	63,445	80,378
Owner occupied	32,797 (61.9%)	39,886 (62.9%)	51,787 (64.4%)
Renter occupied	20,227 (38.1%)	23,560 (37.1%)	28,591 (35.6%)

Source: U.S. Department of Commerce, Bureau of the Census, *Census of Population and Housing* (Washington, D.C.: GPO, 1960, 1970, and 1980).

Indeed, while generalizations are precarious, the total number of vacancies apparently declined in the same ratio.

The most dramatic gains were secured in owner-occupied facilities, but the increase in rental units was nearly proportionate. For both sectors, the magnitude of housing production represented an avalanche. The net absolute growth in year-round units during the decade between 1970 and 1980 (nineteen million) nearly doubled the equivalent for the previous decade (eleven million). These rates of production marked the pinnacle of America's "Golden Housing Era."

This huge increment in availability permitted an enormous upgrading of the housing inventory—and a vast increase in the number of persons who were able to maintain separate housing accommodations (Table 2.2). Average household size declined as the size of the nation's housing inventory leaped ahead of the increase in population. The housing system was able to absorb the unique conjunction of demographic phenomena that we now refer to as the "baby boom." Simultaneously, it provided room for the

Change, 1960–1970		Change, 1970–1980	
Number	%	Number	%
10,346	17.7	19,725	28.7
11,115	19.6	18,979	28.0
10,421	19.7	16,933	26.7
7,089	21.6	11,901	29.8
3,333	16.5	5,031	21.4

creation of new household types and a new structure of housing demand. Whereas, in 1960, each one thousand Americans represented itself in 300 housing units, in 1980 each one thousand was spread among 365 housing units. Per capita housing consumption had increased by 20 percent in twenty years.

Inflationary Explosion and Income Stagnation

Contrary to prevailing economic theory, the dramatic increase of the nation's housing supply was accompanied by disproportionate increases in the costs of homeownership (Table 2.3). Some of this disproportionate increase was a function of outside elements, especially higher energy costs, but the magnitude of the difference was too great to be explained by one or a few specific variables. The price of ownership that had coincided with the Consumer Price Index (CPI) through the mid-1970s suddenly developed its own dynamic. On the other hand, rent levels clearly lagged behind the CPI. As general inflation accelerated during the 1970s, home-

Table 2.2

Changes in Household Composition, 1960, 1970, and 1980
(Numbers in Thousands)

Households	1960		1970	
	Number	%	Number	%
Total	52,799	100.0	63,401	100.0
Family households	44,905	85.0	51,456	81.2
Married-couple family	39,254	74.3	44,728	70.5
Other family, male householder	1,228	2.3	1,228	1.9
Other family, female householder	4,422	8.4	5,500	8.7
Non-family households	7,895	15.0	11,945	18.8
Householder living alone	6,896	13.1	10,851	17.1
Households of two or more persons	999	1.9	1,094	1.7

Source: U.S. Bureau of the Census, Current Population Reports, Series P-20, No. 363, *Population Profile of the United States: 1980* (Washington, D.C.: GPO, 1981).

Note: Numbers may not add because of rounding to one tenth of 1 percent.

ownership costs accelerated almost twice as fast as rents. In short, rents systematically lagged behind ownership costs, irrespective of the rate of inflation.

The impact of the changes in housing prices must be viewed within the context of equivalent changes in median family income (Table 2.4). The real gains in income in earlier decades—the 37.6 percent increase, for example, of the 1950s and the 33.9 percent increment of the 1960s—gave way in the early 1970s to stagnancy, and then to actual decline. From 1973 through 1982, real incomes declined by 10 percent. When these data are compared to the increases in housing cost indexes, the pressures become evident. The marked increments in the supply of housing were mismatched to the relative rise in housing prices and the apparent decline in housing buying power. The coexistence of these several

1980		% Change	
Number	%	1960–1970	1970–1980
79,108	100.0	20.1	24.8
58,426	73.9	14.6	13.5
48,180	60.9	13.9	7.7
1,706	2.2	0.0	38.9
8,540	10.8	24.4	55.3
20,682	26.1	51.3	73.1
17,816	22.5	57.4	64.2
2,866	3.6	9.5	162.0

factors represented a major change in the foundations of the housing market.

Housing ownership is widely understood to be a major goal for most American households. The rapid expansion of the ownership supply in the latter 1970s, however, represented more than an expression of this basic value. It was a response to the pressure of inflation, and it was facilitated by the last waning period of long-term fixed-rate mortgage availability. The vast middle class of America, including in many cases singles and previously atypical householders, fled to the financial refuge of ownership in increasing numbers (Table 2.5).

The very improvements in the supply and distribution of housing *as shelter* permitted the emergence of a very substantial *post-shelter housing society*. Housing became defined as much by its

Table 2.3

Consumer Price Index, for All Items, for Housing, and for Energy,
1960, 1965, 1970, 1975, 1980, and 1982

	All Items	Home Ownership	Rent	Fuel Oil and Coal	Gas and Electricity
Year					
1960	88.7	86.3	91.7	89.2	98.6
1965	94.5	92.7	96.9	94.6	99.4
1970	116.3	128.5	110.1	110.1	107.3
1975	161.2	181.7	137.3	235.3	169.6
1980	247.0	314.0	191.6	556.0	301.8
1982	289.1	376.8	224.0	667.9	393.8
% Change					
Period					
1960–1965	6.5	7.4	5.7	6.1	0.8
1965–1970	23.1	38.6	13.6	16.4	7.9
1970–1975	38.6	41.4	24.7	113.7	58.1
1975–1980	53.2	72.8	39.5	136.3	77.9
1980–1982	17.0	20.0	16.9	20.1	30.5
1960–1980	278.5	363.8	208.9	623.3	317.2
1960–1982	325.9	436.6	244.1	748.8	399.4

Source: U.S. Department of Commerce, Bureau of Economic Analysis, *Survey of Current Business* (Washington, D.C.: GPO, 1960, 1965, 1970, 1975, 1980, and 1982).

Note: 1970 to 1979--Wage Earners and Clerical Workers (CPI-W); 1980 and 1982--All Urban Consumers (CPI-U).

value as a vehicle for speculation and as a hedge against inflation as by its historic value as a refuge from the elements. The move of tenants from rental facilities into their own homes has been one important manifestation of this dynamic.

The Renter-Owner Bifurcation

The flight to ownership has resulted in a rental sector that is increasingly dominated by different, newer household types: households with female heads of working age and single-person households. Typically, these households have lower incomes and less wealth than the more traditional household types who, generally, have moved to homeownership. These renters constitute households that are relatively worse off than households that own their own homes and than renters of the previous decade (Tables 2.6

Table 2.4

Median Family Income, 1950–1982

	Median Family Income	
Year	Actual Dollars	Constant 1982 Dollars
1950	3,319	13,318
1960	5,620	18,317
1970	9,867	24,528
1973	12,051	26,175
1980[a]	21,023	24,626
1982[a]	23,433	23,433

	Change in Family Income	
Period	Constant 1982 Dollars	% Change
1950–1960	4,999	37.5
1960–1970	6,211	33.9
1970–1980	98	0.4
1970–1973	1,647	6.7
1973–1982	−2,742	−10.5

Source: U.S. Bureau of the Census, *Current Population Reports,* Series P-60, No. 127, "Money Income and Poverty Status of Families and Persons in the U.S.: 1980 (Advance Data from the March 1981 Current Population Survey)" (Washington, D.C.: GPO, 1983).

[a]Based on Householder Concept.

through 2.8). This rental sector cannot tolerate high rents, and even the comparatively modest rent increases experienced during the last decade have proven to be a burden. This sector alone cannot guarantee the rental supply sufficient return to remain vital and attentive to high standards of performance.

In short, the rental sector has become defined in large part by households that, whatever their tenure preferences, simply lack the financial capacity to provide themselves with ownership. Affluent households that might previously have chosen to rent have found their preference too expensive in a structure of taxes and inflation that usually favors ownership. Consequently, the pool of renters has become comprised more and more of households who are not "making it" within the general economy. As a result,

Table 2.5

Owner- and Renter-Occupied Units: Household Composition by Age of Head 1970 and 1981 (Numbers in Thousands)

| | Renter Occupied | | | |
| | | | Change | |
	1970	1981	Number	%
Total occupied	23,560	28,833	5,273	22.4
Two-or-more-person households	17,171	18,685	1,514	8.8
Male head, wife present	12,759	10,822	-1,937	-15.2
Under 25 years	2,282	1,822	-460	-20.2
25 to 29 years	2,408	2,380	-28	-1.2
30 to 34 years	1,531	1,701	170	11.1
35 to 44 years	2,154	1,741	-413	-19.2
45 to 64 years	3,148	2,115	-1,033	-32.8
65 years and over	1,236	1,063	-173	-14.0
Other male head	1,143	2,418	1,275	111.5
Under 65 years	1,010	2,297	1,287	127.4
65 years and over	132	121	-11	-8.3
Female head	3,270	5,444	2,174	66.5
Under 65 years	2,899	5,033	2,134	73.6
65 years and over	370	411	41	11.1
One-person households	6,389	10,149	3,760	58.9
Under 65 years	4,109	7,228	3,119	75.9
65 years and over	2,279	2,921	642	28.2

Source: U.S. Department of Commerce, Bureau of the Census, *Current Housing Reports*, Series H-150-79, *Annual Housing Survey: 1981, Parts A and C* (Washington, D.C.: GPO, 1983).

Note: Numbers may not add because of rounding to one tenth of 1 percent.

median rents as a percentage of median income for renter households have risen to troubling proportions—despite the lag in rental increases that would presumably have worked in their favor.

While homeowners have experienced larger increases in absolute income levels, their housing costs have also risen when compared to income. There is considerable anecdotal evidence, particularly concentrated among new homebuyers, of much higher shares of income being devoted to housing. Even for first-time purchasers, however, the financial outlay has been partially com-

Owner Occupied			
		Change	
1970	1981	Number	%
39,886	54,342	14,456	36.2
35,124	45,827	10,703	30.5
30,806	39,137	8,331	27.0
800	887	87	10.9
2,252	3,127	875	38.9
2,938	4,747	1,809	61.6
7,097	8,538	1,441	20.3
13,230	15,330	2,100	15.9
4,490	6,508	2,018	44.9
1,298	2,257	959	73.9
974	1,857	883	90.7
324	400	76	23.5
3,019	4,433	1,414	46.8
2,159	3,425	1,266	58.6
860	1,008	148	17.2
4,762	8,515	3,753	78.8
2,075	4,044	1,969	94.9
2,688	4,471	1,783	66.3

pensated by the sense of accomplishment in securing the American dream, as well as by the capital accumulation and inflation-proofing that it has been possible to gain through ownership. In the case of many owner-occupants, in fact, the very inflation in housing costs, rather than being a sign of misfortune, has become an indicator of the previously mentioned value of homeownership as a pathway to relative wealth and security.

The rental housing market has survived precariously within this turbulence. While renters have increasingly been drawn from the

Table 2.6

Owner and Renter Household Income by Household Composition and Age of Head, 1981

	Median, Owner-Occupied	Median, Renter-Occupied	Ratio of Renter to Owner Income
Total households	$21,800	$11,400	.52
Two-or-more-person households	24,200	13,100	.54
Male head, wife present	25,600	16,200	.63
Under 25 years	19,000	14,100	.74
25 to 29 years	24,300	17,700	.73
30 to 34 years	27,500	17,800	.65
35 to 44 years	30,300	18,600	.61
45 to 64 years	28,700	16,900	.59
65 years and over	13,700	10,000	.73
Other male head	22,300	12,400	.56
Under 65 years	24,800	12,700	.51
65 years and over	13,500	7,600	.56
Female head	13,900	7,800	.56
Under 65 years	14,900	7,900	.53
65 years and over	11,000	8,200	.75
One-person households	8,900	9,000	1.01

Source: U.S. Department of Commerce, Bureau of the Census, *Current Housing Reports*, Series H-150-81, *Annual Housing Survey: 1981, Parts A and C* (Washington, D.C.: GPO, 1983).

pool of the less affluent, nominal rents have grown relatively modestly—and this in the face of rather impressive increases in some of the principal operating-cost components. The degeneration in effective market demand for rental units was surely the root cause, but it was made possible in many cases by a much less broadly acknowledged fact: the existence of relatively inexpensive fixed-rate mortgages. The variety of financing arrangements for multifamily rental housing is much broader than those that have traditionally held true for the one-family equivalent. But at least part of the overall operating situation of income property was buffered by relatively cheap financing costs secured in the past.

Challenges of a New Era

The 1970s was clearly a period in which an unprecedented housing dynamic was forged. The housing inventory expanded by an incre-

Table 2.7

Trends in Relative Incomes of Renters and Owners by Household
Composition and Age of Head, 1973 and 1981

	Ratio of Renter to Owner Income	
	1973	1981
Total households	.63	.52
Two-or-more-person households	.68	.54
Male head, wife present	.73	.63
Under 25 years	.85	.74
25 to 29 years	.83	.73
30 to 34 years	.77	.65
35 to 44 years	.72	.61
45 to 64 years	.74	.59
65 years and over	.80	.73
Other male head	.69	.56
Under 65 years	.66	.51
65 years and over	.65	.56
Female head	.73	.56
Under 65 years	.68	.53
65 years and over	.75	.75
One-person households	1.13	1.01

Source: U.S. Department of Commerce, Bureau of the Census,
Current Housing Reports, Series H-150-79, *Annual Housing Survey:
1979, Parts A and C* (Washington, D.C.: GPO, 1981).

ment almost twice as large as had been achieved in any previous
intercensal period, and new household formation rapidly parti-
tioned the population into an increasing number of smaller and
more varied household formats. The decade will also be remem-
bered as a period when the aspirations of homeownership were
fulfilled. In the beginning of the decade, this was facilitated by
a relatively benign relationship between the cost of acquiring
housing and the level of household income. Toward the end of
the 1970s, inflation increased housing values disproportionately,
thus precipitating additional housing demand for ownership. This
phase marked the maturation of the post-shelter society. Housing
in America became much more important as a form of investment,

Table 2.8

Trends in Rent-to-Income Ratios by Household Composition and Age of Head, 1973 and 1981

	Rent-to-Income Ratio	
	1973	1981
Two-or-more-person households	19.6%	26.7%
Male head, wife present	18.2	22.1
Under 25 years	19.8	24.0
25 to 29 years	17.4	20.0
30 to 34 years	17.0	21.4
35 to 44 years	17.1	21.2
45 to 64 years	16.4	20.7
65 years and over	29.6	30.7
Other male head	21.0	31.1
Under 65 years	20.7	30.7
65 years and over	28.0	33.6
Female head	26.9	40.9
Under 65 years	26.6	40.9
65 years and over	31.0	34.4
One-person households	30.7	31.1

Source: U.S. Department of Commerce, Bureau of the Census, *Current Housing Reports*, Series H-150-81, *Annual Housing Survey: 1981, Parts A and C* (Washington, D.C.: GPO, 1983).

Note: The ratios represent the median rent of each household type as a proportion of the median income of each household type.

as a form of forced savings, and as a refuge from inflation and taxes.

The consequence to the rental market—the loss of much of the more affluent tenantry into homeownership—has raised serious questions as to the long-term economic underpinnings of rental housing. It has also brought into focus the growing income imbalance between owners and renters, a reflection of the increasingly bimodal distribution of income and wealth in the society generally. The housing success of the 1970s and the post-shelter society as a whole was facilitated by mortgage instruments—designed for stable noninflationary economic environments—now extended into a period characterized by strikingly new contours. Fixed-rate mortgages, inadequately reflecting volatile economic conditions, made housing borrowing an unprecedented bargain. But those who supplied funds were left substantially less well off than those who borrowed them. The instability of the economy is no longer conducive to the fixed-rate mortgage, and its continuation cannot be assumed in forecasting future patterns of housing demand and supply.

The overconsumption and speculation that have increasingly characterized America's housing market are products of economic conditions that have largely been swept away. Homeownership no longer is a reliable road to fiscal success, and with the decline in this surety, a substantially new calculus of housing choice will be evidenced. While monetary policy certainly will vary, the absolute priority given housing by our society and embodied in the creation of the protected housing finance industry is at an end. The emerging realities of reindustrialization and overall economic crisis have taken precedence.

The housing surge of 1983–84 has encouraged some observers to hope for a new and long-term upward trend. But the surge has been supported by the successful merchandising of variable-rate mortgages and the development of the secondary market with its competence to tap new streams of financing. These measures, and the ingenuity that has prompted them, may not be reliable in the longer run. They serve to delay the full impact of interest rates due, and they depend on sustained rises in real income in amounts that can be neither predicted nor guaranteed. Thus, the housing recovery is immensely fragile, and has to be placed in context of the extended slump that preceded it and the structural changes that brought it into being.

What has recently been experienced must therefore be read cautiously as the precursor of sustained production stagnation. In such a situation, high ratios of housing expenditure to income would have real, rather than apparent, negative effects. Further reductions in household size would become burdens rather than blessings. Even homeownership itself, stripped of its institutional protection, would again become a financial risk rather than an assured gain. The value of housing would again be defined in terms of shelter, and rental occupancy would once again be highly valued in that regard.

Implications for the Rental Sector

In terms of rent control, half the problem thus resides in the unfortunate demand position of the households that are becoming dominant in the rental sector: households whose composition and income make it difficult to afford even modest increases in levels of rent. At least in the short run, rent control would seem to offer a chance of relief for such households. But if the changes in financial structure, outlined earlier, have any effect in the long run, they will take the form of augmented competition for rental units. At a minimum, households with excess income and mobile life-styles will enter the market for primary and secondary rental "homes," and it is likely that there will be a reemergence, even among the affluent, of interest in housing-as-shelter, as the real costs of ownership become evident and as alternative investments prove to be more satisfying.

The other half of the problem has to do with the ability and the willingness of industry to build rental units, whether for the poor or for the affluent. While vacancy rates are currently rising, there is also a decline in the rental supply. Under circumstances implied in the foregoing analysis, that supply could actually become insufficient to the point of national concern, and an extensive pattern of rent control would do nothing to encourage a return to sufficiency.

With regard to the potential vitality of the rental sector in the years just ahead, several assertions need to be made.

1. The demand for rental housing will increase. The conventional housing forecasts for the 1980s and 1990s were predicated upon the rates of household formation and market penetration that characterized the 1970s. With slight variations, these yielded an approximate average annual net growth of 1.6 to 1.8 million households. Of these (again based upon recent history), approximately one-third would be renters. As suggested above, the level

of household formation, rather than being solely an independent variable, is strongly conditioned by the availability and relative costs of housing. The increased market penetration of homeownership in household configurations that were long the dominant domain of rental facilities may well be the result of economic factors that are no longer relevant.

Within the context of these conflicting patterns, a somewhat slower rate of household formation, but despite this, a much more substantial demand for rental facilities, is indicated. Some of this demand undoubtedly will be absorbed by conversions of now oversized and overcostly one-family houses to multifamily use. But if the pool of potential rental housing stops there, the pressures on the extant supply must yield very substantial inflationary stresses, perhaps combined with a lowering of housing standards. Geographic shifts, both in terms of the movement to exurbia and in terms of persistent interregional flows, indicate the accentuated pressure for additional units. Some rental occupants will view tenancy as a way station toward homeownership, but others increasingly will adapt to a more or less permanent rental housing status. In social welfare terms, the rental inventory will need to expand with or without the public subsidies to which it became accustomed in the 1960s.

2. Private investor interest in rental housing must therefore increase. The departure of private investment capital from the rental housing market and its replacement by a variety of forms of government support do not reflect the commitment of the latter, but reveal the failure of the rental market as a whole to fully engage the interest of investors and entrepreneurs. Now, the change in the depreciation allowances available for rental housing, in concert with an overall reduction in opportunities for tax shelter, has created a new potential. The very shrinkage in alternate real estate investment opportunities within a low-growth economy could leave rental housing as a rare, relatively fresh area of interest. But in order to bring this potential to fruition, the concerns of investors must be clearly comprehended.

Income-producing realty of any form is of interest in terms not only of current yields but also of long-term sales assurance. The need to recapture equity, to maximize leverage, to secure capital gains for alternate investment, or indeed for enlarging real estate holdings, requires such assurance. The value of real estate as collateral is conditioned by ease of transfer. In financial markets that have become increasingly homogenized, with no special reverence or allowances made for residential real estate, the lack of fluidity of tenure in real property becomes an enormous impediment. Millions of dollars of tax-exempt or corporate bonds can be transferred with a telephone call in a matter of minutes. There is no such flexibility in the realty market, nor will it ever be attainable. Thus, ultimate rates of return must be substantially higher in real estate than in more liquid investments.

While this is an age-old problem, in an era of rental scarcity the incentives that are provided for rental housing production will take on new importance, and attention will have to be given to competitive rates of return and the assurance of eventual profits. Public policy toward housing will have to become informed about the ways in which investment markets intersect and will have to become committed to rental housing as a social priority.

3. Condominiums can be seen as a complement to rental facilities. Condominium conversions, as well as the condominium format as a whole, have generally been viewed as competitors to rental facilities. Under present institutional arrangements, this is partly true, but it is conceivable that this successful format could actually enhance the rental situation. This perspective rests on the financial differences between what, in material terms, are often indistinguishable sectors of the housing market. The deductibility of local property taxes, for example, adheres to the owner of a condominium, but it is worthless to both owner and tenant in a rental facility. While, at least in theory, the deductibility of mortgage interest payments is essentially constant for both formats, at present the potential for capital accumulation, to say nothing of capital enhancement, has been available only to the condominium occupant. The latter, in turn, has therefore been willing to pay much more in the way of immediate "rent" for a given housing unit

than holds true for a tenant of such a unit. The very splitting up of ownership under the condominium format has provided a diversification in the financing of such units. What has not been available, however, is the depreciation benefit.

Within this context, a very powerful incentive is available to stimulate investment into construction of rental units. This stimulus is nothing less than a guarantee to the investor of the right to convert rental units, after a given period of operation, into condominiums. Indeed, if the societal pressures for this form of shelter were to increase, the potential of accelerated depreciation, coupled with a minimal holding period of perhaps seven years and insurance against recapture on conversion, exists. The guarantee of at least the potential of conversion would vastly broaden the spectrum of parcel disposition. We would argue, in sum, for a reconceptualization of the entire life-cycle of new rental properties. Tenant purchase and investment by non-residents must be regarded as natural elements of the cycle.

4. Rent control would be an obstacle to such investment incentives because investment in residential rental property faces an enormously competitive financial market. The flexibility of money funds represents merely one end of a spectrum; on the other end there are long-term government bonds at unprecedented yields. Any encumbrance to potential rates of return on, or ultimate disposal of, real property, has these alternative investment outlets to fear. And the threat of rent control could represent such an encumbrance.

The application of the notion of fair rate of return, *a la* the public utility, seems here to be misplaced. The purchaser of shares in a utility may find the nominal rate of return limited, but it has thus far been relatively secure. Further, a glance at the financial problems currently being experienced by some of our major utilities indicates the precariousness of using this analogy. As changes occur in the capital base or releveraging takes place, the very definition of rate of return has altered markedly. Even in areas where investments have been predictable in the past, the term "fair rate of return" may be losing its meaning.

More elusive, and in some ways more basic, is the matter of property interest. As controlled rents deviate further and further from market levels, the nominal tenant clearly develops a property interest in the shelter. Evidence for this situation exists in the many cases where substantial bonuses have been paid to individual occupants in order to empty a building for alternate purposes. The longer rent control is in existence, the greater the gap between contract rent and market rent, the greater the pressures for permanency, and the greater the property-interest bifurcation. This in turn stultifies the final disposition of the occupied parcel. Whether it is for condominium conversion, for nonresidential reuse, or for demolition, the nominal entrepreneur/investor no longer is in control of the property.

Thus, rent control acts as a disincentive to potential investors, whose funds will be required for the construction of rental housing. The smorgasbord of competing investments is far too attractive, and the uncertainties of residential rental properties under rent control are far too worrisome. Once again, the enigmatic quality of rent control rears its head. As a restraint on the housing supply, rent control runs the risk of undermining its own purposes. This is not to say that a negative supply response cannot be compensated by other means, of course, nor is it to belittle the real problems that householders of limited means face in the midst of harsh economic reality. The struggle is to understand and reconcile the negative aspects of rent control, and to locate its proper place in the management of the housing system.

The Model:
Rent Control in New York City

by Michael A. Stegman

At first, it seems absurd that New York City's experience with rent control and regulation is relevant to other communities considering the adoption of such ordinances. After all, New York has almost four times the proportion of units in multifamily structures (that is, with five units or more) as does the nation as a whole, and more than one-third of its apartments are in buildings containing at least fifty units. Two out of three households across the country own their homes but in New York less than three in ten do. In New York more than one in five homeowners lives in cooperatives or condominiums, while across the nation just one in forty does. In short, New York's housing situation seems unique enough to prevent it from being a model for other communities.

Regardless of these differences, New York's almost half century of experience with rent control and regulation has provided the model upon which others are built or against which they are contrasted. Its basic and generic features can be abstracted from the city's unique housing market. This chapter describes New York's situation and then extracts five key issues with which the city is concerned and from which other communities might learn: whether maximum permissible rent increases also become minimum rent increases; why moderate forms of rent regulation do not protect low- and moderate-income families from high rent burdens; the relationship between rent control and underutilization of living space; the difficulty of determining the effects of regulation on the returns to housing suppliers; and rent control as a form of social planning.

Historical Overview

Rent Control

Congress enacted rent control as one of many measures to facilitate the mobilization of the civilian labor force needed by the defense industry during World War II. By imposing a firm ceiling on rents, rent control not only dampened upward price pressures and speculation in the existing housing stock, but also had the effect (then considered salutary) of diverting investment capital from housing into productive sectors of the economy that were more closely allied with the war effort.[1] The Emergency Price Control Act, which initially provided for wartime rent controls, was signed into law by President Franklin D. Roosevelt in early 1942, and rent control was administratively imposed on New York City in late 1943 (see Appendix for a chronology of rent control in New York City).

Although the continuation of postwar rent controls on existing housing could possibly have been justified on the grounds of the extreme shortage that persisted across the country, national policy makers chose to encourage new construction instead. In 1945, all wartime controls on the use of building materials were repealed. To discourage the construction industry from building nonresidential units and luxury housing that offered the greatest profits, President Truman placed a $10,000 price ceiling on all new homes and ordered the Office of War Mobilization and Reconversion to channel no less than 50 percent of all construction materials into housing. In 1945, Truman also created the Office of Housing Expediter to direct a crash program to expand the housing supply.[2] As part of the series of moves to mobilize the nation's productive resources to alleviate the housing crisis, Congress enacted the Federal Housing and Rent Act of 1947 that exempted apartments built after February of that year from all forms of rent control.[3] Thus began the distinction of pre- and post-1947 rental housing in New York City. Under the new law, pre-1947 apartments would be subject to continued controls; new apartments would have totally unregulated rents, and, for the first time, procedures were established for decontrolling rents. These procedures applied almost exclusively to one- and two-family rental structures, however.

With normalization of the national economy, federally administered rent control programs became less necessary and defensible. With the need for continued restraints on rents varying from community to community, the federal government passed on to state and local governments the power to continue, eliminate, or modify the wartime system of rent control. Noting that market conditions continued to be abnormally tight, and vigilance was needed "to prevent 'speculative, unwarranted and abnormal increases' in rents and evictions of tenants during a period of housing 'emergency,' " the New York State Legislature established the Temporary State Housing Rent Commission in 1950 to oversee the system of rent control in New York communities that saw fit to continue their programs.[4]

The extension of rent control in New York City was intended to be a temporary measure justified by continuing housing shortages related to wartime conditions. Increases in the supply of housing through the market were expected to ease price pressures and allow for the elimination of controls. "For this reason, a vacancy rate of five percent was established in the legislation as the criterion for the restoration of a normal supply-demand relationship in the housing market. Anything short of a five percent vacancy rate would be *prime facie* evidence of a continued 'housing shortage.' "[5] In 1955, Governor Harriman further underlined the temporary nature of the state's continued commitment to rent control: "[R]ent ceilings do not bring roofs overhead. Rent control must be viewed as only a single aspect of a broader housing program and as an interim device until such time as an adequate housing supply makes it no longer necessary."[6]

Rent Increases in Controlled Apartments

With the enactment in 1970 of Local Law 30 that created the Maximum Base Rent system (MBR), New York City accomplished the first major reform of its rent control program. The system centers around a formula for computing the maximum base rent for each apartment in a rent controlled building. The MBR approximates the actual rent that would be required to operate the unit under prevailing cost conditions, including generation of enough cash to return 8.5 percent of the equalized assessed value of the building. Rents may be raised by as much as 7.5 percent a year until the MBR is reached for apartments in buildings with no major outstanding code violations, where all essential services are being provided, and where landlords are investing appropriate amounts of money for operations and maintenance.

One way to summarize the effects of the MBR system on rents is through an index whose base period is July 1970, the month preceding implementation of the MBR system. Assuming that an apartment has remained in the rent controlled inventory since then, which means that the same tenant has lived there for eleven years, the approved rent would have increased by 137 percent between 1 July 1970 and 1 July 1981 (Table 3.1). If the increases in rents include the increase for fuel, the approved rent would have increased by 153 percent. From January 1978 to January 1981, the increase, including fuel adjustments, would have been 33 percent.

Rent Stabilization

New York was the only state in the country still administering a rent control program by the end of the 1950s. With growing political conflict between the city and the state over the continuation of controls, the legislature enacted the Emergency Housing Act of 1962, which passed on to the city all responsibilities for administering rent control. Under city administration, buildings erected since 1947 continued to be free of any form of rent regulation until 1969, when the rent stabilization program came into being. (Rents in post-1947 buildings of six or more units were initially exempt from controls by the 1947 Federal Housing and Rent Act. Rent stabilization not only brought these units under a modified form of control but also reinstated controls on rents in decontrolled pre-1947 buildings of six or more units.) While imposition of rent regulation on a previously uncontrolled sector of the rental market was criticized by industry representatives as a

Table 3.1

Schedule of Maximum Allowable Rent Increases for Rent-Controlled Apartments, New York City, 1970–1981

Date	Rent Increase	Rent Index
31 July 1970	--	100
1 August 1970	15.0%[a]	115
1 January 1972	7.5[b]	123.63
1 January 1973	7.5	132.90
1 January 1974	7.5	142.86
1 January 1975	7.5[c]	153.58
1 January 1976	7.5	165.10
1 January 1977	7.5	177.48
1 January 1978	7.5	190.79
1 January 1979	7.5	205.10
1 January 1980	7.5	220.48
1 January 1981	7.5	237.02
1 July 1980[d]	$12.06	
1 January 1981[e]	4.18	

Source: New York City Department of Housing Preservation and Development, Rent Control Division, October 1981.

[a]Represents the first year increase allowed under the MBR law. Provisions: a 15 percent increase is authorized if no 15 percent increase—that is, vacancy increase—had been authorized since 1953. If one 15 percent increase had occurred, an 8 percent raise was allowed, but if two or more 15 percent increases had taken place, none was allowed. Furthermore, if the 31 July 1970 rent was below $60, the increase for four or more rooms was $15, and for one to three rooms, $10.

[b]Represents the annual percent MBR increase. It assumes that in each year the full 7.5 percent can be collected because the MBR had not been met.

[c]A temporary one-year fuel surcharge, collectible for the period 1 July 1975 to 30 June 1976, is not shown. The increase was limited to $2 per room with a maximum of $9 per apartment per month.

[d]The $12.06 represents the average fuel cost adjustment for 1980 that became collectible on 1 July 1980, retroactive to 1 January 1980. The actual increase varies according to type of fuel used and amount consumed; fuel adjustments are not compounded by MBR.

[e]The $4.18 is the average fuel cost adjustment for 1981 collectible as of 1 January 1981. A total of $16.24 is the total average fuel cost adjustment in 1981. Fuel adjustments are computed on an average of 3.4 rooms per apartment.

"shabby betrayal of trust,"[7] city officials justified their actions on the basis of what they deemed to be unconscionable increases in rents by owners of these newer buildings that could not be justified on the basis of cost and that tenants could not afford.

Until 1983, when the State of New York enacted legislation to once again assume full responsibility for administering the rent regulation system, the city's housing agency, the Department of Housing Preservation and Development (HPD), had overseen both the rent control and the rent stabilization systems. Whereas rent control, *per se*, had been a wholly governmental operation, rent stabilization tried to combine industry self-regulation with a complex combination of supervision and control by both governmental and public interest bodies.[8] Sharing the administrative responsibility have been three separate agencies: the Rent Guidelines Board, the Rent Stabilization Association, and the Conciliation and Appeals Board.

The Rent Guidelines Board (RGB) is composed of nine members appointed by the mayor to represent tenants (two members), owners (two) and the general public (five); it was given the authority to establish maximum rates for rent increases for lease renewals and new leases following vacancies.

The Rent Stabilization Association (RSA) is an organization that all owners of apartments subject to the stabilization law are required to join. Its major responsibilities have been: enrolling building owners in the organization; drafting a code regulating the conduct of its membership consistent with the law; and levying and collecting sufficient dues to pay the costs of administering a substantial portion of the rent stabilization system.

The Conciliation and Appeals Board (CAB), the third party that shared rent stabilization responsibilities, was designed to be an independent public agency to enforce the law. Its operating budget was provided by the RSA. Until passage of the State Omnibus Housing Act of 1983, which dramatically overhauled the rent stabilization program, the CAB's principal responsibility was to hear and resolve landlord and tenant disputes arising under the law. While orders of the nine-member CAB (four tenants, four owners, and an impartial chairman) were final and binding on all participants, they were subject to judicial review.

The 1983 Omnibus Housing Act, which placed the regulatory system under the supervision of the New York State Division of Housing and Community Renewal (DHCR), dissolved the CAB and created a state-administered appeals system to hear tenant complaints and rule on landlord petitions for hardship rent increases. With the elimination of the CAB and new restrictions on the RSA that limit the landlord organizations' formal responsibilities to recommending changes in the Rent Stabilization Code to bring it into conformance with the new law, New York City's nearly fifteen-year experiment with rent stabilization as an exercise in industry self-regulation has come to an abrupt end.

The new state-administered rent regulation program has eliminated the New York City Office of Rent Control but retained the RGB unchanged. This board will continue to issue annual rent orders applicable to the city's stabilized stock. The new law has slightly eased the burden of the RGB and has gladdened the hearts of the owner community by eliminating the tenants' as-of-right option to demand a three-year renewal lease. Therefore, the RGB no longer must project operating cost increases three years into a very uncertain future as a basis for making their multiyear renewal lease rent orders.

Another concession to landlords in the new law grants a hardship rent increase to all new owners (who acquired their properties within the past three years) whose gross rental income does not exceed annual operating expenses, including mortgage interest, by 5 percent. These hardship increases are limited to 6 percent in any one year, with the excess spread over subsequent years in similar increments.

From the landlords' perspective such concessions are more than offset by the initiation of a new rent registration system for stabilized apartments. With the beginning of a dwelling-unit-based system of annual registration, both tenants and the regulatory authorities will have specific information on who owns and occupies regulated units, the rents that are being charged for them, and the services that are provided as part of the rental payment. The registration system will make it easier for tenants to determine whether they are being overcharged for their rent-stabilized apartments and for the state more vigorously to prosecute the landlords who exploit their tenants. The law provides that landlords who are found guilty of willfully overcharging tenants can be assessed penalties amounting to triple the rent overcharge for a period of up to two years.

Rent Increases in Stabilized Apartments

Unlike the MBR system, which was designed to eliminate the gap between current revenues and the cost of adequate maintenance, the rent stabilization program was designed to prevent any such gap from arising in the newer stock by permitting landlords to charge economic rents. Under state administration, the stabilization program is still designed to regulate rather than rigidly control rents, and is therefore generally representative of the new generation of moderate rent regulations that many cities have enacted recently to attempt to balance the interests of landlords and tenants. Whether the system operates as it is designed to, of course, is a matter of continuing analysis and debate.

Rent increases for apartments under rent stabilization continue to be determined by the RGB and are issued in a series of annual rent orders. State law requires the RGB to consider the economic conditions of the residential real estate industry; prevailing and projected real estate tax rates; operating, maintenance and labor costs; costs and availability of mortgage financing; the annual supply of housing accommodations; and vacancy rates. In preparing its orders, the RGB issues separate rent increase allowances for one-, two-, and three-year renewal leases with existing tenants and for vacancy leases with new tenants. The vacancy rent adjustment is added to renewal lease increase allowances. Over the past few years, the vacancy lease increases have become progressively larger as the RGB has attempted to shift more of the burden of compensating landlords for rising operating costs from resident tenants to new ones. The 1979 vacancy lease allowance,

Table 3.2

Permitted Rent Increases for Rent-Stabilized Buildings, New York City, 1971-1981

Period	Rent Increase (%)	Rent Index
1 July 1970 - 30 June 1971	--	100.00
1 July 1971 - 30 June 1972	5.4	105.40
1 July 1972 - 30 June 1973	5.4	111.09
1 July 1973 - 30 June 1974	5.6	117.36
1 July 1974 - 30 June 1975	5.6	123.96
1 July 1975 - 30 June 1976	5.3	130.57
1 July 1976 - 30 June 1977	5.5	137.74
1 July 1977 - 30 June 1978	4.2	143.57
1 July 1978 - 30 June 1979	7.7	154.67
1 July 1979 - 30 June 1980	10.3	170.57
1 July 1980 - 30 Sept 1981	11.9	190.92

Source: Table XVI, Explanatory Statement and Findings of the Rent Guidelines Board in Relation to 1981-82 Lease Increase Allowances for Apartments Under the Jurisdiction of the Rent Stabilization Law, 31 July 1981, p. 17.

which was 5 percent more than the increases permitted for renewal leases, rose to 15 percent for leases entered into in late 1981.

The net effects of the different increases permitted each year under rent stabilization can be summarized through a weighted average rent index that takes account of such factors as the mix of lease terms in effect and the extent of tenant turnover (Table 3.2). Between 1971 and 1981, the average rent in a stabilized apartment was permitted to rise by 91 percent. More importantly, perhaps, for the three years between 1978 and 1981, the RGB allowed the average stabilized rent to increase by one-third.

On 24 June 1983, the RGB approved a schedule for maximum permissible rent increases in vacant stabilized apartments, for lease renewals, and for controlled units that were vacated after 1 October 1981. For stabilized apartments in which leases are renewed, rents may be increased by 4 percent if the renewal is for one year, by 7 percent for two years, and by 10 percent for three years. Where there is a turnover in the occupancy of a stabilized apartment, the new rent may be increased by as much as an additional 15 percent, depending upon when the last vacancy in the same unit occurred. Finally, recognizing that a modest percentage increase in permissable rent translates into a very small increase in rental revenues for owners of inexpensive apartments, the RGB issued a special rent order for these units. Owners of apartments renting for $200 a month or less may increase rents by an amount equal to the applicable rent guideline plus ten dollars a month. The RGB estimates that the ten dollar surcharge will apply to about one-fourth of all rent-stabilized apartments.

Vacancy Decontrol and Reregulation

While the city was struggling to reform rent control through implementation of the MBR system, the state once again intervened by enacting the Vacancy Decontrol Law of 1971. Vacancy decontrol partially negated the need for the MBR system by providing for the decontrol of all controlled and stabilized apartments upon a turnover in tenancy. Thus, the rents in a large and growing portion of the inventory were once again permitted to rise to market levels. But just as steeply rising rents and substantial increases in evictions immediately preceded the enactment of the rent stabilization law in 1969, a similar rise in rents among decontrolled and destabilized units led directly to the New York State Emergency Tenant Protection Act of 1974 (ETPA). ETPA modified the concept of vacancy decontrol. Immediately after a market rent was negotiated for a vacated apartment in a previously controlled building of six or more units, the apartment would come under rent stabilization. Vacancy decontrol was terminated altogether for rent stabilized apartments in buildings with less than six units.[9] In 1981, the New York State legislature extended ETPA until 1983.

Summary of Control Status

The rent regulation system now in place in New York City consists of several elements. All apartments built before 1947 whose tenants were in occupancy prior to 1 July 1971 continue to be subject to rent control and the MRB system. All previously controlled and stabilized apartments that saw a turnover in occupancy between 1971 and 1974 were brought up to the then-market levels and entered the stabilization system. All stabilized units that have been continuously occupied prior to 1 July 1971, or that became vacant for the first time since 1 July 1974, remain under stabilization without having their rents brought up to market levels through vacancy decontrol. All apartments in buildings with less than six units that were subject to vacancy decontrol will remain permanently decontrolled and will not come under stabilization. All rent stabilized apartments, whether built before or since 1947, are therefore in buildings with six or more units. Finally, the rents in privately built structures constructed subsequent to the enactment of ETPA in 1974 remain totally unregulated unless they receive some form of public subsidy, for example, real estate tax abatements or exemptions. Such buildings are subject to rent stabilization.

Under the current rent regulatory system, the size and composition of the city's inventory subject to each type of rent regulation will change each year. Because a modified form of decontrol remains in effect, the size of the controlled stock will continue to shrink as turnover in small buildings swells the permanently decontrolled stock and tenant turnover in larger buildings increases the size of the rent stabilized sector. Vacancy decontrol also means that some apartments in older buildings will be subject to stabilization while others will continue to be subject to rent control. New and rehabilitated buildings that receive a public subsidy in the form of tax benefits will add to the stabilized stock, while any new buildings built entirely without public assistance will increase the size of the never-regulated inventory.

The rent controlled sector now accounts for only about 15 percent of the city's occupied rental stock and has experienced a steady decline in recent years (Table 3.3). The decontrolled inventory contains almost as many units as the controlled sector and has grown by 1 or 2 percent per year. With the continuation of the vacancy decontrol program for small buildings, this sector will continue to grow and will soon surpass the controlled inventory in size. Stabilized apartments in pre-1947 buildings make up about one-third of the occupied inventory, which is twice the proportion represented by stabilized housing in post-1947 structures. Low-

Table 3.3

Control Status of Renter-Occupied Housing Units, New York City, 1975, 1978, and 1981

	Number of Units			Change, 1978–1981	
	1975[a]	1978	1981	Number	%
Total	1,999,000	1,930,030	1,933,887	3,857	0.2
Controlled	642,000	402,361	285,733	-116,628	-29.0
Decontrolled	251,000	268,112	282,084	13,972	5.2
Stabilized total	770,000	871,697	928,355	56,658	6.5
Pre-1947	467,000	551,779	615,497	63,718	11.5
Post-1947	303,000	319,918	312,858	-7,060	-2.2
Public housing	165,000	164,765	166,123	1,358	0.8
Other	171,000	223,095	271,593	48,497	21.7

Sources: 1975 data from Lawrence N. Bloomberg, *The Rental Housing Situation in New York City* (New York: Housing and Development Administration, 1976), p. 72; 1978 data from Peter Marcuse et al., *Rental Housing in the City of New York* (New York: Division of Rent Control, 1970), p. 194; 1981 data from U.S. Department of Commerce, Bureau of the Census, 1981 New York City Housing and Vacancy Survey.

[a]Numbers rounded to the nearest thousand.

rent public housing has remained virtually constant and accounts for almost 9 percent of the rental stock. The miscellaneous category, "other," makes up the last 15 percent. Included here are apartments which have never been regulated, single-room occupancy units, federally assisted housing not subject to the rent regulation system, and city-owned *in rem* housing, nearly 34,000 units of which are occupied. Indeed, the expansion of the occupied *in rem* inventory logically accounts for much of the net increase in "other" housing in recent years.

The Level of Rents

Between 1970 and 1981, median gross rents for all occupied units in New York City more than doubled, from $109 a month to $265 (Table 3.4). More importantly, rents increased at a faster rate than the cost of living, with the result that median rents rose by 12 percent in real terms in those eleven years. Rents did not increase steadily, however. Between 1978 and 1981, real rents registered a 5 percent decline. During this time, median rents rose by 26 percent, but the cost of living, as measured by the CPI, rose by almost 33 percent.

Table 3.4

Median Monthly Gross Rent in Current and Constant (1967) Dollars by Control Status, All Renter Households, New York City, 1975, 1978, and 1981

	Current Dollars			% Change	
	1975	1978	1981	1975-1981	1978-1981
New York City	$171	$210	$265	55.0	26.2
Controlled	133	164	213	60.2	29.9
Decontrolled	191	???	271	41.9	22.1
Stabilized					
Pre-1947	176	209	262	48.9	25.4
Post-1947	255	296	368	44.3	24.3
CPI	163.4	192.2	253.9	55.4	32.1

	Constant Dollars			% Change	
	1975	1978	1981	1975-1981	1978-1981
New York City	$105	$109	$104	-1.0	-4.6
Controlled	81	85	84	3.7	-1.2
Decontrolled	117	116	107	-8.5	-7.8
Stabilized					
Pre-1947	108	109	103	-4.6	-5.5
Post-1947	156	154	145	-7.1	-5.8

Sources: 1975 and 1978 data from Marcuse et al., p. 256; 1981 data from New York City Housing and Vacancy Survey.

Note: Rents in current dollars were rounded to the nearest dollar before calculating rents in constant dollars. Rents in constant dollars were calculated by dividing rents in current dollars by the CPI for the appropriate year. Rents in constant dollars were rounded to the nearest dollar. The percentage change was calculated from the rounded numbers.

There are at least three important findings relative to changing rent levels and the control status of housing in New York City. First, median gross rents have risen more rapidly for controlled than for stabilized housing. Since 1975, median controlled rents have increased by 60 percent, whereas median rents in pre- and post-1947 stabilized housing have risen 49 percent and 44 percent, respectively. One reason the stabilized sectors experienced different rates of rent increases, even though the RGB orders apply equally to all stabilized units, is that each is characterized by different mixes of lease terms and tenant turnover rates. The greater the turnover rate and the shorter the lease term, the greater the permissible increases have been under recent RGB rent orders.

Second, controlled rents have actually increased faster than the overall rate of inflation in recent years. This has been due to the combination of 7.5 percent annual rent increases up to the unit's MBR, fuel cost passthroughs, and biennial increases in MBRs of 9 or 10 percent in recent years. In real terms, stabilized rents have declined since 1975 by several percent. Controlled rents have increased by a few percentage points; yet the median rent for pre-1947 stabilized apartments is still $49 higher than for controlled units. This suggests that the MBR system, while keeping rent increases in line with trends in operating costs, still has not accomplished its primary objective of closing the rent gap in the controlled sector that was initially caused by rigid rent ceilings imposed on the stock in 1948 without any provisions for periodic cost-related rent increases.

Third, rent levels vary significantly by control status. Pre-1947 stabilized units rent for 23 percent more than do controlled apartments ($262 versus $213). Similarly post-1947 stabilized units cost 40 percent more than pre-1947 stabilized apartments, although in this case the higher rents signify higher quality housing. Further, decontrolled rents are on the average higher than controlled rents ($271 versus $213 in 1981), although in recent years, controlled rents have increased more rapidly. This is true for the entire period 1975–1981 as well as for the period 1982–1984.

Generic Issues

A Rent Ceiling or a Rent Floor?

As indicated above, roughly 300,000 apartments—15 percent of all occupied rental units in New York City—have been decontrolled. All of these previously regulated units are in buildings containing fewer than six apartments and have been decontrolled upon a turnover in occupancy either as a result of the Vacancy Decontrol Act of 1971 or the Emergency Tenant Protection Act of 1974. Yet, though decontrolled rents tend to be higher than controlled rents, increases in rent are higher among controlled than decontrolled units. This was true between 1975 and 1981, when decontrolled rents rose by 42 percent compared to 60 percent for controlled rents. And, it was true between 1978 and 1981, when controlled rents rose by 30 percent compared to just 22 percent for decontrolled rents. One wonders why.

There are several plausible explanations for the differences in rates of rent increase, including location, building size, and owner residency. With respect to location, decontrolled units are more likely than either rent-controlled or stabilized apartments to be in Brooklyn. More than half of the decontrolled inventory is in Brooklyn, and it is there that median rents for all housing have risen the least. Because they contain fewer than six apartments, moreover, decontrolled buildings are much more likely than others to have their owners in residence. This implies that owners of decontrolled buildings are less likely to manage their properties solely for maximum profit. Resident owners are more likely than nonresident owners to invest their own labor in maintenance on which they do not seek a monetary return, to screen potential tenants to assure compatibility with themselves, and to increase rents only upon a turnover in occupancy. Thus, the fact that owners reside in over half of all decontrolled and in just 15 percent of all controlled buildings may explain a substantial portion of the difference in rates of rent increase experienced by the controlled and decontrolled sectors in the recent past.

There is a more interesting hypothesis to consider, however, and while it cannot be rigorously tested with available data, it deserves serious attention. The proposition is that in the controlled market maximum permissible rent increases automatically become minimum actual rent increases. If this were true, then a system of administered price increases that reduces individual landlord uncertainty about market conditions could have the unintended effect of raising housing costs to consumers in softer submarkets where market rents might actually be lower than the maximum permitted by law.

The pattern of rent increases in New York City between 1975 and 1981 indicates that the difference between the two rates of rent increase for controlled and decontrolled housing widens during periods of high inflation and narrows when operating-cost pressures decline. It may be that only after an official determination of the extent of operating costs changes, and the sanctioning of substantial rent increases during inflationary and generally uncertain economic times, do owners of regulated apartments feel sufficiently confident of their market strength to raise their rents to the legal maximum. Thus, for example, between 1975 and 1978, when the CPI for the New York Metropolitan Area rose by 18 percent, decontrolled rents in real terms remained virtually unchanged, while real controlled rents increased 5 percent. From 1979 through 1981, when the CPI soared by nearly one-third, both market sectors lost ground to inflation but decontrolled rents fell by about 8 percent in real terms and controlled rents dropped only 1 percent.

The fuel-adjustment program is another reason why regulated rents in New York City have increased more rapidly than unregulated rents during periods of inflation. Under the adjustment program begun in 1980, up to 75 percent of the increased cost of heating fuel has been passed on to tenants in the form of higher rents. In 1980, more than 236,000 rent-controlled tenants received fuel-cost-adjustment rent increases averaging over twelve dollars a month, or $145 for the year. At the median controlled rent, this amounts to an additional rent increase of 5.7 percent. By October 1981, another fuel-cost-adjustment rent increase averaging over four dollars a month had been implemented. If these two fuel passthroughs were deducted from the median 1981 controlled rent, the average increase from 1978 to 1981 would fall to 20 percent, which is slightly below the 22 percent increase in decontrolled rents for the same period.

The High Rent Burden

Among the many purposes of rent control and stabilization programs is the protection of low- and moderate-income households that are spending an excessive amount of their income on housing. Of course, if the rent regulations allow rents to be adjusted periodically according to the CPI or some other measure of changes in operating costs, rent control is not likely to offer much protection

Table 3.5

Median Gross Rent-to-Income Ratio, All Renter Households, New York City, Selected Years

	1950	1960	1965	1968	1970	1975	1978	1981
Median gross rent-to-income ratio	18.9%	18.7%	20.4%	21.0%	20.0%	24.7%	28.4%	28.0%

Sources: Data for 1950–1978 from Marcuse et al., p. 197; data for 1981 from New York City Housing and Vacancy Survey.

to tenants whose incomes are not similarly indexed to inflation. Indeed, while median rents in New York City increased by 143 percent between 1970 and 1981, the income of renters grew by just 54 percent. Given that the cost of living rose by 114 percent in New York City over this period, real rents increased by 12 percent while real income fell by nearly 30 percent. Consequently, the median gross rent-to-income ratio for all households increased by 40 percent since 1970 alone, from 20 percent to 28 percent of income (Table 3.5).

Even with rent regulation, almost half of all tenants now spend at least 30 percent of their incomes for rent and utilities. This group has grown considerably since the late 1960s (Table 3.6). In 1981, three of every ten renters in New York City actually spent 40 percent or more on rent, an 83 percent increase since 1968. This group includes 41 percent of all elderly households and at least half of all households in New York with incomes below $6,500 a year.

Because of the changing characteristics of the renter population and the housing inventory, it is very difficult to assess the policy significance of these recent changes in housing expense burdens. Increases in rent-to-income ratios can reflect the loss of higher-income families to the homeownership market, a disproportionately high rate of growth in traditionally poor socioeconomic groups, across-the-board stagnation in incomes, substantial rent inflation, or combinations of these factors. Also, some of today's higher nominal rents may be attributable to increases in the quality and amount of space that families buy.[10] Nevertheless, the analysis does suggest that the more serious challenge to creating

Table 3.6

Percentage of Households with Rent-to-Income Ratios over Specified Levels, New York City, Selected Years

Gross Rent-to-Income Ratio	1950	1960	1965	1968	1970	1975	1978	1981
25% or more	n.a.	n.a.	34.9	37.2	35.5	49.1	57.1	56.6
30% or more	25.0	25.0	25.3	27.4	n.a.	38.1	46.3	45.6
35% or more	n.a.	19.0	18.7	21.2	23.2	30.8	38.0	37.1
40% or more	n.a.	n.a.	14.5	16.7	n.a.	25.2	31.6	30.5

Sources: Gross rent-to-income ratios 25% or more, 30% or more, and 35% or more, 1950-1978, Marcuse et al., p. 198; gross rent-to-income ratios 40% or more, 1965 and 1968, from Niebanck, pp. 149-50; 1981 data from New York City Housing and Vacancy Survey.

and maintaining a healthy rental market in the foreseeable future might have to do with the adequacy of income rather than the unresponsiveness of rent regulations to the cost of doing business.

Overcrowding and Underutilization

The long-term decline in household size in New York City means that overcrowding now plagues a relatively small proportion of renter households. Using the traditional measure of overcrowding—more than one person per room—only 7 percent of all rental units in New York City would be described as overcrowded. Now at a stable level, the present incidence of overcrowding is less than half of what it was in 1960 and 20 percent lower than it was in 1975.

It is frequently argued that rent control contributes to a misallocation of dwelling space by discouraging mobility and thereby inhibiting normal adjustment of housing space to changes in household size. This would be especially true for so-called empty nesters, householders whose grown children have moved away. Paul L. Niebanck tested the space allocation hypothesis for New York City in 1968 by defining a set of occupancy standards that related household size to living space. He determined that 20 percent of all renter households were overcrowded in 1965, and that 16 percent of the units were "underutilized," that is, relative to the number of occupants and according to the standards he employed, were unnecessarily large (Table 3.7).

Replicating Niebanck's analysis with 1981 data indicates that

Table 3.7

Overcrowding and Underutilization in Renter-Occupied Housing Units by Control Status, New York City, 1965 and 1981[a]

	Overcrowding		Underutilization	
	1965	1981	1965	1981
All renter occupied	20.2%	14.1%	16.0%	19.7%
Controlled	17.0	7.3	18.7	26.5
Decontrolled	18.5	8.1	25.5	38.3
Never controlled	14.2	--	10.2	--
Pre-1947 stabilized	--	20.5	--	12.2
Post-1947 stabilized	--	16.1	--	12.1

Sources: Niebanck, *Rent Control*, Tables V-4 and V-5, pp. 133, 135; Stegman, *The Dynamics of Rental Housing*, pp. 116-18.

[a]Niebanck defined the following occupancy standards:

Household Size	Overcrowding	Normal Occupancy	Under-utilization
1 person	1 room	2-3 rooms	4 or more rooms
2 persons	1 room	2-4 rooms	5 or more rooms
3 persons	1-3 rooms	4 rooms	5 or more rooms
4 persons	1-3 rooms	4-5 rooms	6 or more rooms
5 persons	1-4 rooms	5-7 rooms	8 or more rooms
6 or more	1-5 rooms	6 or more	indeterminate

overcrowding has declined from 20 to 14 percent, while under-utilization has increased from 16 to 20 percent of all households. In the controlled stock, underutilization has increased from 19 percent of all households in 1965 to 27 percent in 1981, and in decontrolled apartments, from 26 percent to 38 percent. Under-utilization rates in both pre- and post-1947 stabilized sectors were 12 percent in 1981, or between one-half and one-third of the rates in controlled and decontrolled apartments.

The analysis suggests that tenants in controlled housing continue to occupy more space relative to their household size than do renters overall. The greatest degree of underutilization, however, in 1965 and 1981, was in decontrolled housing, which tends to be more spacious than other market sectors. Rent regulation does appear to contribute to the phenomenon of underutilization, but the overriding variable seems to be the persistent decrease in household size. The median size of renter households in New York has fallen from 2.2 to 1.9 persons since 1965. In Manhattan, in fact, half of all renters live alone. Small households, regardless of the control status of their housing, are likely to have "excess space," while disproportionate numbers of large families continue to live in overcrowded apartments throughout the housing market.

Rent Stabilization and Fair Return

Unlike the MBR-based rent control program, New York City's rent stabilization regulations make no explicit provisions for assuring landlords of the opportunity to earn a fair return. Presumably units are being rented at market levels when they enter the system and the annual rent orders of the RGB will permit landlords to maintain market rents. It is very difficult, however, for the RGB to test the accuracy of its assumptions against market realities. While it is relatively easy to compare the RGB's annual rent orders with changes in the CPI or U.S. Bureau of Labor Statistics (BLS) price indexes, these comparisons are analytically meaningless because different rates of rent increases apply to renewal leases of different durations, while vacancy adjustments only apply to units that have turned over. The aggregate rent impact of the RGB's annual orders on a given building or a given landlord will depend upon the actual mix of lease terms in effect, the proportion of expiring leases that will be renewed, and the turnover rate. The average weighted rent index of stabilized rents referred to earlier embodies the RGB's assumptions concerning the distribution of current leases and the turnover rate.

Based on a field study done in 1976, the RGB assumes a 25 percent, 20 percent, and 55 percent distribution of one-, two-, and three-year leases, respectively, in the stabilized sector. The same field survey estimated an annual turnover rate of 18 percent, a rate that the RGB uses to translate its annual rent orders into an average rent increase throughout the stabilized stock. While the 1981 Housing and Vacancy Survey results indicate that the actual distribution of lease terms in effect varies from the RGB estimates, the differences tend to offset each other so that the actual average lease term (2.2 years) and the one assumed by the RGB (2.3 years) are almost identical.

In contrast, the estimated 18 percent turnover rate greatly exceeds the actual 1981 citywide rate of just over 10 percent. This means that a substantially lower number of stabilized apartments are eligible to receive the generous 15 percent vacancy lease adjustment that the RGB permits for new leases. The actual rents resulting from the RGB's most recent order will be less than it intended. Moreover, since the Housing and Vacancy Survey indicates that turnover rates vary dramatically by borough, even though operating and capital costs do not, the rent effects of the RGB's orders will be uneven.

In addition to the weighted rent index, the RGB uses changes in the operating and maintenance (O and M) ratio to assess the reasonableness of the allowed rent adjustments for new leases in stabilized apartments. The O and M ratio is the percentage of rent that owners allocate to operating and maintenance costs. It is an important indicator of the economic state of the rental housing industry because the higher the ratio, the lower the percentage of the rent roll that is available to cover vacancy losses and rent arrears, mortgage costs and profits. High O and M ratios present very difficult operating choices to owners of rental housing, especially during periods of rising interest rates, when financing for multifamily housing, and older properties in particular, is either not available or is available only at very high rates and for very short terms.

According to the RGB, average O and M ratios increased by about 27 percent during the period 1971 to 1981, and by 11 percent between 1978 and 1981 alone (Table 3.8). This recent sharp increase can be compared to the more gradual 15 percent increase in the index over the first seven years of the rent stabilization program, during which time the prices of operating inputs were rising much more slowly than in recent years. To the owner, these O and M increases mean that, holding constant the quality of building operations, the proportion of the rent dollar available to cover vacancy losses, pay debt service and return a profit has declined from 45 percent to 30 percent. In assessing the significance of this steady rise in the O and M burden, the RGB noted in 1980 that as long as the rent increases it grants generally reflect the magnitude of actual increases in O and M costs, owners' net income will remain constant while their O and M ratios will rise.

Table 3.8

Operating and Maintenance Cost-to-Rent
Ratio for Rent-Stabilized Buildings, New
York City, 1972-1982

Period[a]	O & M: Rent Ratio
1971	0.55
1972	.55
1973	.56
1974	.62
1975	.62
1976	.64
1977	.65
1978	.63
1979	.64
1980	.68
1981	.70

*Source: Explanatory Statement and
Findings of the Rent Guidelines Board in
Relation to 1981-82 Lease Increase Allowances for Apartments Under the Jurisdiction of the Rent Stabilization Law*,
31 July 1981, p. 17, Table XVI.

[a]Periods run from 1 July through
30 June.

From the owner's perspective, a passthrough of all O and M cost increases translates into a constant cash flow but a real decline in the profitability of a building.

Rent Control as Social Planning

Rent control is a form of social planning in that it involves public intervention in the private market in order to achieve social welfare objectives. To the extent that it substitutes public housing decisions for private housing decisions, a properly designed and effective rent control program requires that the administering agency have substantial knowledge of the local housing market and access to large quantities of high quality housing data. The magnitude of this challenge and the incompleteness or inaccuracy of data may lead to inappropriate policy choices. Reference to two particular aspects of the New York City experience will illustrate this point.

First, it will be recalled that periodic rent increases are permitted to landlords of rent-controlled and rent-stabilized housing and that these are determined by two different processes. Depending upon whether their apartments are currently renting at their respective MBRs or not, owners of rent-controlled housing may increase their rents by 7.5 percent a year up to the MBR. The MBR is adjusted every two years, based on the results of a field study of changes in operating costs for controlled housing.

In contrast to this relatively straightforward process is the far more subjective one used by the RGB to determine the rent adjustments that will be permitted for stabilized units. Annual rent increase orders of the RGB rely heavily on estimates of changes in the prices of operating inputs (not expenditures) in rent-stabilized buildings. These estimates of price changes are based on annual surveys prepared for the city by the BLS. Despite these surveys, however, there is still substantial disagreement between owners of stabilized buildings and the RGB, and between the RGB and tenant organizations, over whether the RGB relies too little or too much on the BLS data, what the specific relationship is between price changes and actual landlord expenditures, and how much beyond O and M costs the RGB should go in making its annual rent decisions. One of several areas of disagreement with the RGB's current procedures concerns its estimates of two- and three-year inflation rates. These rates are necessary components of the RGB's multiyear-lease rent increase orders. In the RGB's own words, "forecasting price changes is not an exact science."[11]

In its recent rent orders, the RGB has tended to compensate landlords for rising operating costs and past underestimates of inflation and soaring financing costs by permitting higher vacancy rent increases rather than lease renewal rent increases. As indicated earlier, one of the RGB's latest rent orders included a 15 percent vacancy allowance. The RGB approved the large vacancy allowance as a "means of compensating for the drastic rise in mortgage financing costs" and chose the vacancy allowance over the usual rent guidelines increase procedure to "minimize the burden on tenants in occupancy."[12] The apparent reasons for allocating the additional rent burden to new tenants are that movers are in a better position than tenants in place to trade off the higher costs against their need for space and quality and that movers tend to be more affluent than nonmovers.

This is not the case, however. The 1981 Housing and Vacancy Survey of the New York City housing market indicates that recent movers in the rent-stabilized sector have lower incomes than do rent-stabilized households who have not moved for several years. The median income for households who have been in the same stabilized apartments for at least five years was $20,900 in 1980, compared to $19,200 for households who moved into their present apartments in 1978 or 1979. In contrast, households who moved into their present units in either 1980 or 1981 had a median income of just $17,100. Similarly, recent movers are more likely than nonmovers to suffer high rent burdens. Fully one-fourth of them had to pay at least 40 percent of their income for their new apartment.

Second, it is also informative to recall the set of special actions that the RGB has taken to help prevent low-rent units from dropping out of the housing stock or falling into such seriously deteriorated condition as to become uninhabitable. In 1983 the RGB issued a guideline that included an extra rent increase that would apply to all apartments then renting for less than $200.[13] That same year, it granted an additional ten dollar increase to all units renting for less than $250. The RGB's actions were taken in recognition that the base guidelines (4 percent, 7 percent, and 10 percent for one-, two-, and three-year lease renewals) did not represent sufficient return to keep up maintenance levels. In other words, the RGB decided that beyond its formal and "objective" market intervention, it should intervene still further to accomplish an additional public purpose.

Similarly, and also in 1983, the RGB issued a special rent increase for apartments with long-term occupancy. Units experiencing no vacancy since 1975 were granted the basic guideline increase plus 15 percent. In this case, the RGB acted so as to correct, partially, a market imbalance that it had in fact helped to create. By choosing to help landlords catch up with inflation, through vacancy rent adjustments, the RGB acted against the interests of new tenants and actively encouraged residential stability. Then, having discouraged mobility, the board found that owners of apartments with stable occupancy were being undercompensated for certain costs not covered by the base guidelines. So it created an addition to the guidelines to correct for the omission.

Social planning in the United States has typically acted as a mediator between market forces and public needs. At their rhetorical limits, proponents of free enterprise might postulate that the two are synonymous, and proponents of collectivism might hold that the two are irreconcilable. The real struggle has typically been found somewhere between these poles, and rent control is an example. In New York City, decades of adjustments and readjustments have left many observers wondering whether a satisfactory reconciliation can be found. The terms and conditions of rent control have been changed through time. New rules have been instituted to compensate for the unintended consequences of old rules. The program has successively been extended and contracted in efforts to govern potential abuses, to induce positive behaviors, or to influence factors that otherwise would have the power to erase the desired social ends. At one time or another, every conceivable issue has shown itself in New York City, from the criteria for decontrol to the definition of adequate return, from the relevance of the vacancy rate to the possibility of discriminatory treatment.

In contrast to the longitudinal analysis of New York City, the California experience is a cross-sectional representation of the rent control phenomenon. There experimentation with rent control has been less a series of adjustments through time, and more a range of independent experiments, each responding to its own unique set of political and social circumstances. Rent control in California presents new evidence of the comparative value of the "invisible hand" and the "visible hand" in providing adequate housing services to the population, and it also provides a new perspective by which the conflicts and responses in New York City can be viewed.

Appendix. Chronology of New York City's Rent Regulation System

1942   President Franklin D. Roosevelt signed the Emergency Price Control Act, the enabling legislation establishing wartime rent controls.

1943   Rent control was administratively imposed in New York City.

1947   The Federal Housing and Rent Act of 1947 exempted apartments built after February 1947 from national rent control.

1950   The New York State legislature passed the Emergency Housing Act of 1950 that established the Temporary Rent Commission to oversee New York City's rent control system.

1962   The Emergency Housing Act of 1962 gave New York City the responsibility of administering its rent control system.

1969   Rent stabilization began in New York City. Rents in buildings built after 1947 and previously decontrolled units in buildings of six or more units were brought under rent stabilization, a modified form of rent control. The Rent Guidelines Board, Rent Stabilization Association, and the Conciliation and Appeals Board were established to administer rent stabilization.

1970   New York City Local Law 30 was enacted, creating the Maximum Base Rent system and introducing the concept of economic rent to the city's rent-controlled stock.

1971   The Vacancy Decontrol Law of 1971 was adopted, providing for the decontrol of all controlled and stabilized units after a change in tenancy.

1974   The Emergency Tenant Protection Act terminated vacancy decontrol for rent-stabilized apartments and required that vacated rent-controlled units in buildings of six or more units come under rent stabilization after a free market rent (subject to tenant challenge as excessive) is negotiated with the new tenant.

1981   The Emergency Tenant Protection Act was extended until 1983.

1983   New York State once again assumed full responsibility for administering New York City's rent regulation system. The state legislation became fully effective on 1 April 1984.

Dispersion and Adaptation: The California Experience

by W. Dennis Keating

Shortly after New York City abandoned rigid rent controls and enacted rent stabilization, new interest in rent regulation began to be expressed across the country. The California experience is representative of the range of public responses, and this chapter chronicles and interprets that experience. The chapter begins after the debate over the merits and demerits of rent control itself.[1] Attention is given to the current status of the program, particularly the administrative and legal aspects, and to its future prospects. A central theme emerges: Is California—or, implicitly, any state— justified in preempting the right of localities to enact rent controls? In that regard, several alternatives to rent control are considered, in terms of their comparative value in assuring affordable housing to renters.

The Evolution of Local Policy

According to the California Department of Housing and Community Development (HCD) 1,435,000 lower-income California renters (37 percent of all renters) were paying more than one-fourth of their incomes for rent in 1981.[2] HCD noted that the "inability of increasing numbers of households to afford suitable housing" was the state's most widespread housing problem, with half of all California renters paying more than they can actually afford.[3] This conclusion contributes to the debate over what is an acceptable rent-to-income ratio. While California still adhered to the 25 percent rent-to-income ratio as the standard of affordability under state housing programs at the time the HCD claim was made, the federal government in 1981 had increased its standards for tenants in federally assisted housing to 30 percent.[4]

While increases in rents generally lagged behind inflation and tenant income in the early 1970s, this situation has recently begun to change. In many areas, rents have kept pace with inflation, and tenants' real incomes have declined.[5] Between December 1978 and December 1982, for example, rent increases virtually equalled the overall inflation rate in the San Francisco Bay region.[6] Lower-income tenants were especially hard hit. To what extent most tenants can afford rent increases and just how much they can afford remains controversial, but it is at least an interesting coincidence that several Bay Area cities adopted rent regulation during the post-1978 period.

Another source of concern is the decline in new housing construction. The tight rental housing market prevalent in California is attributable largely to that decline. HCD estimated that 315,000 units would be needed annually through 1985 to meet the state's housing needs.[7] Only 210,000 units were constructed in 1979 and 145,000 in 1980, however, and in 1981 new housing production plummeted to 105,000.[8] In none of the three years did the proportion of multiples exceed 43 percent. While precise data are lacking on the types of new multiple-unit housing being built, the United States General Accounting Office (GAO) reports: "[T]he majority of multi-family housing units currently being built are either (1) subsidized, (2) high-rent, or (3) condominiums."[9] To the extent that this pattern holds true in California, most tenants would be unable to afford either new market-rate rental housing or condominium housing.[10] The national administration's insistent cutbacks in federal housing assistance and the budgetary restrictions that inhibit California's state and local governments from providing adequate housing subsidies mean that there will not be enough new subsidized rental housing built to meet the needs of those lower-income tenants who cannot find affordable existing apartments in the unassisted market.

The problems of insufficient supply and unaffordable rents are reflected jointly in the pattern of vacancy rates. In many California housing markets, rental vacancy rates have fallen below the traditional norm of 5 percent. Data on rental vacancy rates in California are usually based on postal surveys, conducted for the Federal Home Loan Bank Board and the United States Census Bureau, and while they, too, are subjects of criticism, there is little disagreement about the general situation or the trend in recent years. Indeed, the California phenomenon is but one manifestation— albeit a relatively serious one—of a national rental housing problem. Disagreements over its nature and extent are many,[11] but while these disagreements continue, numerous California communities have considered and adopted local rent control.

A Variety of Responses

As a result of an initiative to amend the charter, California's first local rent control ordinance since World War II was enacted in 1972 in Berkeley. Its enactment led almost immediately to a series of legislative events and judicial responses. In 1976, the California Supreme Court upheld the right of local government to enact rent control, under the police power, to alleviate serious housing problems. That same year the California legislature banned local rent control, but Governor Brown's veto sustained the principle of local option.

Further interest in local rent control was propelled by the aftermath of the 1978 Proposition 13 property tax reform initiative. While sponsors of the statewide measure promised tenants a share of the benefits from reduced property taxes, most landlords not only declined to provide voluntary rent rebates but actually increased rents. Well-publicized efforts were made by Governor Brown and the state's largest landlords to convince owners to roll back rents to pre-Proposition 13 levels or pass property tax savings on to tenants. But these efforts failed, and the legislature rejected a proposal to mandate a partial rebate. Tenant protests ensued, and demands were made on local governments to enact rent control.

In May 1979, a public opinion poll revealed widespread support for rent control. Fifty-six percent of the Californians polled favored rent control while 21 percent opposed the measure. Moreover, 73 percent of the tenants (who constitute a majority of householders in the state) favored such a measure; 20 percent opposed it.[12] This sentiment was not immediately translated into law in all instances, however. In many communities, especially the suburbs, rental housing problems are not seen as critical, especially where tenants constitute a minority of the population. Moreover, rent control has been resisted by most local governments where it has been proposed, and real estate industry representatives have strongly opposed rent control in every instance.

Nonetheless, by 1984 thirteen populous California localities had adopted rent control laws of one kind or another: the county of Los Angeles; the city/county of San Franciso; the cities of Berkeley, Beverly Hills, Cotati, East Palo Alto, Hayward, Los Angeles, Oakland, Palm Springs, San Jose, Santa Monica, and West Hollywood.[13]

In addition, thirty-one localities have mobile home rent control ordinances.[14] Mobile home rent control ordinances typically establish rent review commissions that arbitrate rent disputes between mobile home park operators and tenants. Finally, at least three California localities have considered the adoption of commercial rent controls, and in 1982 Berkeley became the first California city to enact such controls.[15]

Many of California's 429 incorporated cities and 58 counties have considered the adoption of residential rent controls but have rejected them. The voters of 25 cities and counties have defeated thirty proposed rent control initiatives since 1977. Five of these initiatives would have required landlords to rebate part of their Proposition 13 property tax savings to tenants. The most prominent defeats of rent control initiatives occurred in Berkeley (1977), Long Beach (1980), Los Angeles County (1983), Oakland (1980, 1982 and 1984), Pasadena (1981), San Diego (1980), San Francisco (1978 and 1979), Santa Barbara (1978), Santa Cruz (1979, 1980 and 1982), and Santa Monica (1978).[16] In contrast, Berkeley (on four different occasions), Cotati, Davis, Hemet (mobile home), Palm Springs, Santa Monica, Thousand Oaks, and West Hollywood have enacted rent control by initiative.

Two of the Berkeley initiatives and the Cotati, Davis, Palm Springs, and Santa Monica initiatives have subsequently been ruled unconstitutional. Thus, the status of rent control is far from resolved, whether in specific local jurisdictions or in the courts. The situation is volatile, but in a short time, California has moved into second place—after New Jersey—in terms of the number of localities that have adopted rent control measures.

The Issue of State Preemption

State governments have three alternatives in dealing with local rent control: (1) they may preempt, reserving to the state the exclusive authority to regulate rents;[17] (2) they may permit local option rent control, but require adherence to state-legislated guidelines;[18] or (3) they may allow unrestricted local rent control, subject only to judicial review.[19]

Subsequent to the flurry of effort in 1978 and 1979 to establish statewide oversight, California has reinforced its tradition as a strong home rule state. In 1980, a coalition of California real estate industry groups placed on the ballot an initiative to restrict local rent control. This proposed constitutional amendment would have invalidated all existing local rent control legislation and required mandatory referenda for its adoption. Any local rent controls adopted thereafter would have had to conform to state-wide standards. The most important of the proposed restrictions were these: (1) annual rent adjustments would have been allowed, equal to the annual increase in the Consumer Price Index (CPI); (2) vacated apartments would have been exempt from rent increase ceilings; (3) single-family residences would have been exempt; (4) rent controls would have been administered by appointed committees rather than elected boards; and (5) no just cause eviction requirement would have been required.

The initiative would also have blocked rent rollbacks and registration of controlled units, as well as other features of the more restrictive local laws sponsored by tenant advocates. The highly controversial measure was resoundingly defeated, 65 percent to 35 percent.[20] Additional attempts to pass state preemption legislation failed in 1983 and 1984. California still therefore has no mandatory state standards of its own governing local rent control.[21]

The exception to this general rule, of course, has to do with certain federal and state preemption for subsidized housing. In 1975 the United States Department of Housing and Urban Development (HUD) issued regulations prohibiting the application of local rent control to privately owned, federally subsidized rental housing,[22] and in 1975 the California legislature exempted all rental housing assisted by the California Housing Finance Agency (CHFA) from local rent control.[23]

Broader proposals to condition the eligibility of localities for some federal housing assistance on eliminating or restricting local rent control have been introduced in Congress, and in April 1982, the President's Commission on Housing recommended the adoption of such a preemption policy.[24] In 1983 Congress partially preempted the application of state and local rent controls applicable to the newly authorized Rental Housing Rehabilitation and Development Program.[25] While broader federal rent control preemption remains a possibility, California localities are currently free to regulate the rents of privately owned rental units, except for those subsidized or insured by HUD or CHFA.

Strong, Moderate, and Weak Controls

It is inadvisable to generalize about the cost, administration, impact, and legal status of California's rent controls because their legal form varies so considerably.[26] Moreover, the coverage, stringency, and enforcement methods of rent control often vary according to the relative political influence of organized landlords and tenants at the local level. Analytically, it is useful to describe them in terms of the criteria that the state government itself has identified: (1) statement of legislative intent; (2) vacancy rate required to justify rent control; (3) exemptions; (4) appropriate administrative agency to implement; (5) criteria for determining hardships; (6) rent increase criteria; (7) vacancy decontrols; (8) adjustment of base rents; (9) method of implementation (via initiative, referendum, or local ordinance); and (10) duration and termination.[27] Employing these criteria, one can categorize the local experience according to whether the controls are "strong," "moderate," or "weak."

Santa Monica and Berkeley have prototypically strong rent control laws. Both resulted from voter-approved initiatives drafted by tenant groups, and both have broad coverage of units, mandatory registration, annual rent increase adjustments based on increases in operating and maintenance expenses, and administration by an elected board. Neither city allows for decontrol of vacant apartments, and termination of rent control can occur only if the rental vacancy rate returns to an established norm. In addition to rent and eviction controls, Santa Monica's law includes demolition and condominium conversion controls, administered by an elected rent control board. This provision is unique in the United States.[28]

Berkeley's current law is modelled after Santa Monica's but does not cover demolitions or condominium conversions. From its inception, Berkeley's rent stabilization program has faced well-organized landlord opposition. In 1981, a landlord-supported slate won five of the nine seats on the city council. With this working majority, the administration of rent control was transferred from a tenant-backed group to a landlord-supported group of appointed rent stabilization board commissioners.[29] Amid continued turmoil, Berkeley has subsequently voted (in 1984) to strengthen its law and to replace the appointed board with an elected board.[30]

Moderate rent regulation characterizes the ordinances in Los Angeles (the city), San Francisco, and San Jose. Passed into law by council action, these ordinances are less restrictive than those—like Santa Monica's or Berkeley's—proposed by tenant advocates and enacted by voter initiative. More limited in their coverage, these laws provide for automatic annual general percentage rent increases unrelated to landlords' cost increases. They permit the decontrol of vacant units, temporarily allowing a landlord to charge a market rent, which is again subject to controls after reoccupancy. They use an approach to rent adjustment appeals by landlords and tenants that emphasizes mediation and a more flexible definition of a fair return for landlords. And they originally included sunset clauses; that is, explicit provision was made for automatic termination of the program.

Both strong and moderate rent control programs typically exempt newly constructed apartments and allow landlords to pass the costs of capital improvements on to tenants. The rent control laws characterized as moderate have no ceilings on passthrough costs and vacancy allowances, whereas both Santa Monica and Berkeley impose annual overall ceilings of 15 percent on all allowable rent increases and make them conditional on landlord compliance with housing and health codes.

While San Francisco has twice refused to restrict vacancy decontrol or require landlords to register, it has strengthened tenant protection, requiring landlords to apply for prior approval of any rent increases over the percentage guideline. Initially, tenants had to appeal individually in order to challenge such increases. Los Angeles requires landlords to register, allows them an automatic annual rent increase, exempts luxury rental and single-family units, and permits the temporary decontrol of vacated units. In early 1982, after a heated but inconclusive controversy over vacancy decontrol, Los Angeles extended rent control indefinitely. Later that same year, it decided against amending its charter to permanently exempt new construction from rent control. And San Jose has made it unanimous among major moderate rent control cities by extending its ordinance indefinitely.

Oakland and Los Angeles County have what can best be called weak rent controls. Oakland's rent arbitration law resembles the moderate forms of rent regulation just described, but it has allowed much higher annual general rent increases and it does not contain the just cause eviction provision that is included elsewhere. In reviewing tenant appeals of landlord rent increases exceeding its ceiling, Oakland's rent arbitration board has generally approved much larger increases than allowed in other localities.[31] Oakland voters have thrice rejected rent control initiatives. Los Angeles County has also allowed very high rent increases, and decontrols are permitted on all vacated units. Los Angeles County decided to phase out rent control in 1983, but then extended it in the face of a much stricter tenant initiative, which was later defeated.

Mobile home rent control is the weakest form of rent control found in California. Twenty-eight California cities and three counties have enacted mobile home rent controls, in addition to localities whose regular rent controls cover both apartments and mobile homes. Usually these ordinances simply allow mobile home tenants to appeal any rent increases to a commission appointed by the governing body of the jurisdiction to arbitrate disputes, but often without any specific guidelines or formulas.

Some observers have maintained that, once adopted, rent control policies would inevitably become stricter, due to tenants' political pressure,[32] but so far this has not happened uniformly. While some ordinances have been strengthened (for example, San Francisco), several cities (including Davis and El Monte) did not extend their initial temporary measures, and the interpretation and administration of Berkeley's law changed dramatically after landlords won an electoral victory in 1981. On the other hand, landlord-sponsored initiatives designed to weaken rent control have been rejected in Santa Monica and Berkeley. Thus, the fortunes of rent control have waxed and waned with landlords and tenants gaining and losing, in turn.

Administrative Particulars

Only fragmentary information concerning the administration of rent control is available, because local rent control boards generally operate quite independently and because no systematic evaluation has been attempted by the state or another outside party.[33] For comparative purposes, however, we have tabulated the differences among rent control in Los Angeles (city), San Jose, San Francisco, and Santa Monica on several scales, as of March 1982 (Table 4.1).

In California, funds to finance the cost of rent control administration can come either from a locality's general fund or from landlord and tenant fees for registration and appeals. These fees are typically quite modest, on a per-unit basis, except in jurisdic-

Table 4.1

Selected Aspects of Local Rent Control Administration in California, 1982

City	Controlled Rental Units[a]	Annual Registration Fee Per Unit	Budget for FY 1980-81	Size of Staff	Landlord and Tenant Petitions[b]
Los Angeles	472,000	$ 7	$2.7 million	70	7,470
San Jose	52,000	3	253,000	5	3,354
San Francisco	unknown	none	194,000	9	5,034
Santa Monica	16,000	72	2.6 million	50	1,790

Source: Author's inquiry of administering agencies, 1982.

[a]Numbers are approximated   [b]Cumulative total

tions that have adopted strong rent control. Santa Monica's disproportionately large tenant-paid fee, which is also reflected in its
budget and staff size, reflects the very high costs of legal defense
of an ordinance that has been subject to repeated challenges in
court. As long as rent control is administered entirely through
landlord and tenant fees, it presents no significant financial burden
to localities, and it therefore requires no state assistance.

Legal and Analytical Clarifications

Numerous constitutional challenges to rent control have been filed
with the California courts, paralleling in many ways property
owners' suits challenging land use regulation under California's
Environmental Quality Act, the state's Coastal Protection Act, and
local ordinances governing condominium conversion and land
development.

The leading case is *Birkenfeld v. City of Berkeley*,[34] in which
the California Supreme Court upheld the right of a local government to enact rent controls in order to deal with serious rental
housing problems. But the court also ruled Berkeley's 1972 rent
control initiative unconstitutional, holding that its individualized
procedures for rent adjustments violated landlords' rights to due
process. The local initiative measure had not allowed annual general rent adjustments, and its procedures for making individual
adjustments had been too cumbersome.

This decision left unanswered many legal questions that the

courts are now addressing. In *Carson Mobile Home Park Owners' Association v. City of Carson*,[35] the California Supreme Court upheld the validity of a mobile home rent control law challenged as violating the court's *Birkenfeld* standards.

The court will next deal with the complex question of defining what it meant in *Birkenfeld* when it ruled that rent-controlled landlords are entitled to a "just and reasonable return on their property." Landlords and tenants usually disagree as to what constitutes a fair return on the landlord's investment, as reflected in controlled rents. Various fair return formulas have been devised, but the courts have failed to define clearly what they consider to be a fair return.[36]

In 1983 and 1984, the California appellate courts considered the fair return issue in three cases involving mobile home rent controls (San Juan Capistrano, Oceanside, and Los Angeles), and in two other cases (Cotati and Berkeley).[37] In 1984, in *Fisher v. City of Berkeley*, the California Supreme Court upheld the constitutionality of Berkeley's rent control ordinance and provided additional guidance as to what constitutes fair return.[38] The courts may also be called upon to address a set of related issues in which case judicial review will continue to impose limits on the scope and application of local rent control in California.[39]

Studying the Impacts

In these early stages of rent control, it is difficult to judge its impact on the local housing market.[40] Good data do not exist; rent control laws and circumstances change; and analytical problems abound. Few programs have been motivated to investigate their own effects, and few investigators have been ready to undertake the task. Despite these difficulties, there have been several studies of local rent control in California. Together, they address, with varying degrees of confidence and consistency, many of the important issues.

The Rand Corporation conducted a study of rent control in the city of Los Angeles and concluded: (1) there is no demand-induced rental housing crisis, since the rental vacancy rate is almost normal; (2) tenant mobility has declined; (3) some rental units have been removed from the inventory; (4) there have been slight reductions in maintenance; and (5) new production has not been reduced.[41] Rand's finding of "no crisis" was quite controversial, partly because a previous UCLA study had concluded that the city's rental vacancy rate was virtually zero.[42]

Another study of the impact of rent control on Los Angeles concluded that the benefits of rent control were inversely related to income, that benefits have been unfairly transferred from landlords to tenants, and that rent control will impede new construction to the detriment of tenants.[43] Los Angeles, faced with these conflicting studies, extended rent control indefinitely, and commissioned an empirical impact study of its own. This most recent study (Los Angeles, *1984 Rental Housing Study*) found that rent stabilization translated into an average monthly rent savings of $7 or $18, depending on the basis of comparison that was used. It also discovered that "by far the most important determinant of which tenants are subsidized and which pay premiums (under rent stabilization) is the length of time that a household has remained in its rental unit" (pp. 4–6). Finally, it concluded that the net effect of rent stabilization was to move more households into, than out of, the affordable range.

In reviewing the Santa Monica rent control program and its impact in connection with court litigation, UCLA economist David Schulman concluded on behalf of the city that, between 1978 and 1980, the nominal values of rent-controlled apartments increased as a result of allowable rent increases, although real values declined because landlords lost potential additional income.[44] Landlords' experts claimed that considerably greater value reductions had already occurred because of rent controls and projected even larger ones in the future.

An opinion poll by the California Public Interest Research Group (CALPIRG) found that Berkeley tenants generally observed little, if any, change in their building and maintenance services after a year of rent control.[45] This study did not measure actual changes in the maintenance of Berkeley's rent-controlled housing, however, so its conclusions are not fully objective or definitive.

The impact of vacancy decontrol is a question that has been of considerable interest to researchers. A UCLA study found that in Los Angeles, annual rent increases in vacated units averaged 18 percent, compared with only 8 percent for units without any tenant turnover.[46] In 1982, Los Angeles refused to institute permanent decontrol of vacated units. According to a city planning department survey, median rents for vacated units in San Francisco increased by 30 percent in 1980.[47] In 1981 and 1983, Mayor Feinstein's vetoes ensured that no ceilings were imposed on rent increases for vacated units in San Francisco.

Rent control's impact on new construction has also been of interest. One comprehensive study has tried to assess the impact of rent control on housing supply. After considering the situations in six California cities, the study concluded that rent control is reducing the number of available rental units by deterring new construction and by encouraging demolitions and condominium conversions.[48] Unfortunately, the study was done shortly after the institution of rent controls, too soon to assess the full impact.

California now requires local redevelopment agencies to report on their activities to the local governing body annually,[49] and it would seem worthwhile to extend such a requirement to local rent control boards. Such mandatory annual reports would provide more systematic data on the scope, administration, cost, and impact of local rent controls, without imposing serious fiscal burdens on localities. In 1984, the Berkeley Rent Stabilization Board commissioned a study of regulated landlords and tenants to ascertain their knowledge of the law and the board's policies and their attitudes toward rent control.[50] This study could serve as a prototype for local studies elsewhere.

Rent controls in California may have been in effect long enough now to justify a statewide survey of their particulars. The Office of Planning and Research has performed a similar survey of condominium conversion controls (locally regulated), and the Department of Housing and Community Development

(HCD) has done likewise on the relocation activities of local re-development agencies (state-regulated). A systematic state-commissioned study that would assess the impact of rent control could provide valuable data needed to inform the debate.

Alternatives to Rent Control

Even the most ardent advocates of rent control generally acknowledge that controls do not constitute a lasting or comprehensive solution to the rental housing problem. They agree on the need for substantial increases in the supply of affordable rental housing to meet the persistent demand. Instead of vastly increasing, however, California's production of new multifamily housing has declined drastically in recent years. The HCD describes the situation, with bureaucratic restraint, as "a very tight supply of rental units."[51] Moreover, most new unsubsidized multifamily housing is too expensive for most of California's tenants.

The recent escalation of costs has been associated primarily with very high mortgage interest rates and sharp inflation in the price of land. Restrictive land use and environmental regulations have put additional pressure on costs.[52] Still another factor has been the increased dedication requirements and fees charged for new housing developments that have been imposed by local governments since the passage of Proposition 13 in 1978.[53]

Both the Governor's California Housing Task Force in 1979 and the Governor's Task Force on Affordable Housing in 1981 recommended measures to promote the construction of affordable housing, and subsequently many of them have been adopted by the California legislature. Effective in 1979–1980, state law now requires regional planning for fair share housing,[54] provides density bonuses,[55] permits the vesting of development rights,[56] and restricts growth controls.[57] These measures have been complemented at the local level, where there has been experimentation with inclusionary zoning as a way to provide more affordable housing.[58]

In 1979, recognizing the critical need for subsidized housing, the state appropriated $100 million for a rental housing construction program.[59] The state also authorized several new forms of mortgage finance to encourage more capital investment in housing,[60] and it has attempted to persuade public employees' pension funds to invest in affordable housing.[61] In view of the state's recurrent fiscal problems, however, it is not likely to commit additional funds to subsidize new or existing rental housing. For example, in fall 1984, Governor Deukmejian approved some modest funding for state housing programs, but he also vetoed several housing measures to promote the construction and rehabilitation of low- and moderate-income rental housing.

Local governments, whatever their good intentions, are suffering from cutbacks in both federal aid and state Proposition 13 bailout funding. Localities have not used tax-exempt mortgage revenue bonds effectively to finance affordable multifamily housing, largely because of the prevailing high interest rates. As interest rates decline, this form of housing finance could become more important, unless of course the federal or state government further restricts its use. San Francisco and Santa Monica have pioneered in the use of land use controls to require the developers of major downtown commercial projects to subsidize affordable housing.[62] While some affordable housing can still be built through the innovative combination of available housing subsidy programs, tax incentives, and regulatory policy, this cannot satisfy the current and projected demand for affordable rental housing.

At the national level, and as an alternative to the regulatory approach, there have been signs of a revival of interest in direct government subsidies for low-income housing. The President's Commission on Housing has advocated such an approach[63] and has recommended the conversion of HUD's Section 8 housing assistance program into a housing voucher system providing direct rent subsidies to low-income tenants.[64] But, similar to the state level, announced intentions and actual performance have not matched. The needs of California's lower-income renters, as documented by HCD and confirmed in the Rand study, are therefore not being met.

In short, for various internal and external reasons, state and local efforts have not been able to provide affordable housing. In the absence of greater subsidies, California localities may choose increasingly to rely on regulation to preserve the existing supply of moderately priced rental housing. In addition to rent controls, as such, condominium conversion controls, demolition controls, and limitations on the conversion of hotel rooms and apartments may become even more common.[65] Berkeley and Santa Monica already have demolition controls, and in 1979, San Francisco became the first city in the United States to regulate the conversion of single-room occupancy (SRO) residential hotels to preserve them as affordable housing. Berkeley and San Francisco also regulate the conversion of apartments into commercial uses in certain districts.[66] Even in areas where housing markets are comparatively open or public policy has been relatively conservative, some degree of public intervention into the affairs of rental property owners may be in the offing.

For example, voluntary landlord-tenant mediation boards have been established in at least twenty California localities including Alameda County and the cities of Mountain View, Palo Alto, Sacramento, Santa Cruz, and San Diego.[67] Quite effective in many areas of dispute, these bodies typically have difficulty resolving issues related to rent increases. Hence, rent arbitration, which is the approach followed in the moderate and weak forms of California rent control, may be considered when housing market conditions in these localities show signs of worsening.

Conclusions

California's rental housing problem will undoubtedly grow worse in the short run, but there is considerable debate as to the depth and dimension of the problem. The 1980 UCLA and 1981 Rand studies of Los Angeles, previously described, provide dramatically contrasting assessments. The same contradictory perspectives hold at the national level. A 1981 HUD study found no current national shortage of rental housing,[68] but reports by the U.S. General Accounting Office and the National Urban Coalition concluded that the nation's rental housing conditions are worsening.[69] Confusion regarding trends in such underlying factors as interregional migration, financial markets, and household formation rates only exacerbates the policy dilemma.[70]

What can be said with some certainty is that, where local housing markets are typified by very low vacancy rates and abnormally high rent increases, and where tenants organize politically, rent control will be considered at least as a temporary measure. California, as one state in which these conditions are common, will thus continue to experience local rent control on a fairly widespread basis. The key policy choice—whether and in what way the state should intervene—may rest on whether rent control occurs only in what are largely the tightest or most oppressive local markets and on whether housing markets experience problems that are attributable to rent control. Were rent control to become adopted in situations where the matter is one of the redistribution of privileges, as such, there would then be logical reason for state intervention on the side of restraint. If, contrariwise, intense suffering were to be experienced in areas where its victims did not have the political strength to institute rent controls, the state would have reason to create its own form of protective rent control. Landlord, tenant, and local government lobbying, as well as judicial decisions, will undoubtedly be the dominant political influences in the legislature's deliberations over the rent control preemption question. California will be well advised to consider the experience of those eastern jurisdictions that have previously faced this perplexing policy issue. New York City is a primary area of observation,[71] and New Jersey is another.[72]

Meanwhile, any state experiencing extensive rent control would benefit from careful monitoring of local activity within its own boundaries. It might require local annual reports by rent control agencies, and it also might consider commissioning a statewide survey of local rent controls and their impact.

An Analysis of Intercity Rents

by John I. Gilderbloom

Rent control is primarily concerned with the level of rents. In theory and in popular understanding, rents themselves are the product of the intersection of housing demand and housing supply. But demand and supply, in turn, are dependent on the structural features and idiosyncrasies of local housing markets. This chapter identifies the factors that are associated with higher levels of rent and that cause a demand for rent control.

Supply-Side Explanations

Earlier chapters have alluded to the reluctance of local officials to introduce rent control. While ideological factors have entered the picture on occasion, most controls have been instituted as a straightforward response to real or anticipated rent increases and to the hardship that they impose on households of modest means. Proponents of rent control have been aggressively alert to the recent general rise in rents, after a period of stagnation, and to the resultant increase in rent-to-income ratios among the least affluent sectors of the population. Further, they decry the situation wherein the high cost of housing makes it impossible to afford other basic necessities.[1] The question is: What are the best ways to address the problem? The answers are several: income guarantees, subsidized housing production, rent control, or other market reforms. Whatever the avenues for relief, they presumably could be more easily evaluated and compared if the sources of rental increases were better known.

The most generally accepted explanation of the variation in levels of rent among local housing markets appears to reside in the relative quantity of housing. In his widely cited book, Glenn H. Beyer states:

> Although there is usually a close relationship between price of housing and costs of construction, price in the local market is a direct reflection of the relationship between supply and demand. As stated earlier, if the supply is large, relative to demand, the price of dwelling units (including rents) will tend to be lower; conversely, if the demand is large, relative to supply, house prices will tend to be higher. For older houses, current price levels are more important than cost of construction. . . . The most common measure of the degree of balance between supply and demand, both quantitatively and qualitatively, is the number and type of dwelling units that are vacant and available.[2]

That is, when landlords are truly in competition with one another, the reasoning goes, rents are held to what would be described as reasonable levels. Whenever the vacancy rate falls below a critical level, on the other hand, a shortage is seen to exist that causes rents to be excessively high.[3]

Economists are not alone in their view that the vacancy rate is the key variable for determining whether there is a housing crisis. Indeed, this viewpoint is shared by government officials, builders, bankers, and landlords. Even tenant leaders have pointed the finger at supply factors as the cause of the housing crisis.[4] Nationally known tenants' rights lawyers have spoken forcefully on the matter:

> It has to be said somewhere, where it will stand out, so why not here: The heart of the tenant's problem is not the laws and regulations (imperfect though they may be), nor the goodness or badness of landlords (for they, like you, are but human)— no, the heart of the problem is with the supply of housing. It is drastically short.[5]

The mere fact that cities typically require a housing emergency to be defined in terms of the vacancy rate in order to justify rent control to themselves and to the courts reveals the importance of supply conditions. In Los Angeles, opponents and proponents have each relied on a set of vacancy statistics to prove their case:

> The differences are important to a climactic battle scheduled at the City Council today over the future of rent control. Landlords and tenants have been taunting each other during months of public hearings, with each side citing its favorite statistics. . . . The different figures have been used by one side to argue that Los Angeles renters face an extreme housing crisis that is critical for low-income residents, and by others to show that the market is only slightly tighter than the national average. The whole ballgame in rent control is measuring the vacancy rate. . . .[6]

And in Miami Beach, where rent control has been enacted and repealed during the last decade, the fate of the issue has hung on the rental vacancy rate: "Five percent is a kind of turning point, under which you would seriously consider rent control . . . [That is] the general figure that has been used nationwide."[7] Kenneth Baar and Dennis Keating have found in a survey of twelve selected rent control statutes that virtually all cite the "housing shortage" as a justification and reason for enacting rent control.[8] The Santa Monica rent control law, well known for its comprehensiveness and restrictiveness, is a prime example. There the conditions that define a housing emergency are specified in detail:

> A growing shortage of housing units resulting in a low vacancy rate and rapidly rising rents exploiting this shortage constitute a serious housing problem affecting the lives of a substantial portion of those Santa Monica residents who reside in residential housing. . . . If the average annual vacancy rate in any category, classification, or area of controlled rental units exceed five (5) percent, the Board is empowered, at its discretion and in order to achieve the objective of this Article,

to remove rent controls from such category, classification or area. . . . If units are decontrolled pursuant to this subsection, controls shall be reimposed if the Board finds that the average annual vacancy rate has thereafter fallen below five (5) percent for such category, classification or area.[9]

Similar provisions are contained in other rent control ordinances. The New York City law still relies on the 5 percent rule, and in other cities, while occasionally the number is set at 3 percent, the language in every surveyed case refers either explicitly or implicitly to the limited supply of affordable housing as the underlying rationale for rent control.

Housing Filtration

Associated with the idea that the vacancy rate determines the overall price of housing is the long-standing theory of housing filtration.[10] In its simplest form, the theory portrays the housing supply as passing, incrementally, from high-income occupancy to lower-income occupancy. The process begins with new construction of housing at the upper-income level, is sustained by progressive obsolescence and relative price decline, and encouraged by a complementary rise in income at each level of the society. The process continues until it touches the lowest-income families, allowing the lowest quality housing supply to be abandoned altogether or upgraded to what are essentially "new" housing opportunities for upper-income demanders. The aggregate result is described as an advance in housing well-being for each population sector and an improvement in the quality of the housing stock as a whole.

According to housing filtration theory, new housing units are built because of technological obsolescence, style obsolescence and deterioration, and because supply conditions create profit opportunities sufficient to attract new investment capital. Profits are therefore a key indicator of market health; they must be attractive enough to sustain the process. New construction, induced by profitability, benefits everyone along the chain, in terms of housing quality, housing choice, and the levels of relative rent.

Proponents of filtration as a normative theory are understandably critical of local and state government actions that constrain the supply of new housing. They argue that because of government restrictions and regulations, housing is not being built in sufficient quantity to prevent housing prices from soaring. Without such restrictions, they assert, supply would be able to respond freely to demand, and prices would stabilize at acceptable and reliable levels.

These arguments are restated in the recent report issued by the President's Commission on Housing. The report calls for free and deregulated markets, reliance on the private sector and minimal government intervention. Arguing that only the very poor have a housing problem, the commission finds that the high housing costs they confront are, in substantial part, a function of government regulation. It goes on to suggest that the following federal, state, and local regulations should either be abolished or modified:

> housing construction standards, environmental restrictions, Davis-Bacon wage requirements, the Federal Flood Insurance Program, municipal rent control and condominium/cooperative conversion laws, and local land-use policies. . . . It [government] should also encourage a stable economic environment for homebuilding by reducing restrictions on the industry and terminating excessive regulation of land development and housing production. The free market would then be able to provide housing at lower prices and thereby make housing more widely available.[11]

This viewpoint is shared across political party lines. President Carter's Task Force on Housing Costs correlated local regulations with high housing costs, and its argument closely resembled that of President Reagan's commission:

Since the early 1970's, however, the problem of rising housing costs has been greatly exacerbated by two other factors— growing environmental and land-use regulation and the fiscal difficulties of many American communities. Communities have slowed their growth and new housing development has been restricted. These new factors that have quickened the pace of rising housing costs portend a long-term problem for the future unless major steps are taken. [12]

In arriving at their conclusions, both President Carter's and President Reagan's task forces relied heavily on studies performed by well-known and respected organizations and individuals. [13] It is both logical and widely accepted that supply restrictions affect availability and price. What is not clear is the share of the responsibility for which these restrictions are accountable.

The Role of Market Demand

The supply side does not stand in isolation, of course. Chapter 2 articulated the complex, dynamic, and mutual relationship between supply and demand in its most recent manifestation. Changing housing preferences, spirited by more profound shifts in life-style, abetted by the regional movement of economic opportunities, and facilitated by long-term trends in real income, have had deep and lasting influences on the housing market and derivatives such as the vacancy rate and other outcomes relevant to rent control. These demand factors can usefully be summarized in terms of the extent of population growth or decline in specific local markets.

But, beyond the extent or intensity of demand, it is the supply that seems to be determinant. In his review of empirical studies of housing costs, Michael Ball concludes in effect that, operationally, demand itself can best be expressed in terms of supply. He identified three categories of "demand variables": (1) locational advantages such as the distance from home to work or school; (2) house characteristics that measure the number and type of interior features; and (3) environmental aspects that represent the quality of the area—population density, green belts, pollution, crime, and architecture. According to Ball, the "argument is that if one house has more desirable attributes than another, this higher consumer valuation will be reflected in a higher market price."[14]

Most of the studies on levels of rent have neglected interurban variations. Exceptions exist, and these too are informative.[15] Here, several new variables appear to have independent influence. David Russell Wheeler has found that rent varies according to the kinds of business activity within a city, and that rents tend to be higher in cities with corporate headquarters than in cities that are mostly industrial. Richard P. Appelbaum found, in his study of one hundred urban places, that rents in the United States are positively correlated with location outside the South, as well as with population growth rate and median family income. Conversely, he found that rents are negatively correlated with age of city and percentage of units in single-family structure.

Intercity Rent Differentials

The scholarly work to date has pointed toward the need for an analysis that simultaneously incorporates three dimensions: a broad range of apparently relevant variables, rather than one or a few; a set of localities that can be compared through time, rather than a single city focus at one moment in time; and a methodological tool that can accommodate a large number of behavioral interactions. The balance of this chapter provides such an analysis. By means of a linear multiple regression exercise, the impacts of both supply and demand factors on rents are studied, among an array of relatively autonomous housing markets.

The analysis includes all urban areas in the contiguous forty-eight states that could, in the base year, be regarded as relatively self-contained housing markets. Specifically, this means any urban area containing one central city of at least 50,000 population, at least twenty miles distant from the nearest other urban place. The 1970 census lists 134 such cities, standardized for missing data, and the 1980 census shows 144 places. They represent urbanized areas only; no attempt was made to disaggregate markets, geographically or otherwise. This group of areas is drawn from—but expands upon—the data base generated by Appelbaum.[16] He restricted his correlation analysis to cities of less than 400,000 population, and he did not focus on such variables as proportion of rental occupancy, change in size of rental stock, or rental vacancy rate—variables that are directly relevant to the subject of this book.

The research effort is not designed to control for such intracity sources of variation such as have previously been mentioned (locational and environmental aspects, for example) but to measure the supply variables across different housing market areas. The ideal analysis would, of course, account for both inter- and intracity variables, and would include measures of housing quality and amenities, forms of tenure, and the social organization of landlords. At best, the extent of the influence of such factors can only be implied, because they are either not accessible on a comparative basis or simply not recorded.

Although, at this stage, conclusive judgments cannot be drawn, Michael Ball's work is instructive here. In describing his attempt to match variables, he cautioned that, however high a degree of "fit" might be observed between or among them, it is all too easy to draw misleading conclusions. The results presented here will have some significance in the debate over the kind of market interference represented by rent control and will serve as a stimulus for additional research.[17]

The Variables

The variables selected for the study were based on a review of the literature, within the constraints of available data for selected cities. To avoid breaking the statistical rule of having no more than one variable for every ten cases, the number of independent variables was limited to ten in the basic equation.[18] The dependent variable for each equation is median monthly rent for 1970 and 1980 in each of the cities. The independent variables, including those hypotheses that housing economists and urban sociologists would use in regard to them, include:

1. *Rate of population growth*. Rapidly growing cities should have higher rents because of the inability of new construction to anticipate demand. In the rental sector, moreover, landlords might seek to cover the risks that presumably accompany newcomers who have not established permanent employment or credit in the area.

2. *Quality of the rental housing stock* (indicated by both the extent of older units and the proportion of units without adequate plumbing facilities). Units that are either old or lack basic plumbing facilities should tend to have lower rents. A plausible argument could be made, however, that median rents would be higher in areas where such housing is common. The reasoning would be that, given a tight supply, rents for decent housing would be unnaturally bid up, skewing the overall profile toward the high end.

3. *Regional location*. Rents in the South have historically lagged behind rents in other regions. Whether this condition would hold today in light of the economic boom in sunbelt cities is open to question.

4. *Median family income*. In a competitive housing market, median income should not affect rents, once differences are controlled. To the extent that competition is imperfect, however, landlords will be able to charge "what the market will bear," and hence higher income areas will pay higher rents for similar quality housing. At least a mild positive correlation between income and rent should be expected. Whether income would have a stronger influence in high-quality markets than in low-quality markets is uncertain.

5. *Proportion nonwhite*. It is unclear whether large proportions of these population groups should be correlated with higher or lower housing costs. One argument is that because of market discrimination by whites, nonwhites pay higher amounts for rent for the same quality and quantity of housing. An oft-stated and

contrary claim is that when nonwhites live in an area, the aggregate demand for housing falls and housing costs are therefore restrained.

6. *Size of population.* Generally, larger cities should experience relatively higher rents. Analysts make reference to the superior range of amenities and opportunities in larger urban centers, and expect the "price" of such advantages to be paid, in part, through housing.

7. *Rate of new construction.* Many theorists hold that, because new construction reduces scarcity, housing markets with large percentage increases in new rental housing experience lower rent levels in comparison with their slow-growth counterparts. On the other hand, rentals in newly constructed buildings generally tend to be higher than those in the existing inventory.

8. *Proportion of the total housing stock that consists of rental units.* Two plausible hypotheses exist concerning this variable. First, most economists argue that housing markets with a large proportion of rentals would provide tenants with a wider range of choices, leading to a more competitive market and hence lower rents. Cities with a low percentage of rentals would provide fewer options for tenants and correspondingly experience higher rent levels. Second, in cities with high percentages of rental units, more buying and trading occurs, thus making investment in apartments more attractive for the professional landlord, with the result that in cities with high proportions of rental housing higher rent levels are to be expected.

9. *Rental housing vacancy rate.* If the vacancy rate is low, rents can be expected to be high; conversely, areas with high vacancy rates should have comparatively low rent levels.

The Analysis

The variables were taken into account through a linear multiple regression analysis on the dependent variable, 1970 and 1980 median rent. Ordinary least squares were used for estimation, and "F" statistics were used in all tests.

No attempt to specify a full causal model of the determinants of intercity rent was undertaken. Rather, the main focus of the analysis was on the impact of a selected number of factors on rent, taking informal account of other relevant variables found in the literature. The method thus isolates certain factors of anticipated importance and estimates the degree of their apparent influence. The results are examined with reference to the absolute values of the standardized regression (beta) coefficients (Tables 5.1 and 5.2). These coefficients allow comparisons of the relative magnitude of each variable to be made directly. The standardized regression coefficient measures the change in the standard deviation of the dependent variable in relation to the standard deviation change in the independent variable. This statistic allows each independent variable to be compared for relative importance. The larger the absolute value of the independent variable's beta coefficient, the greater the variable's importance in explaining variation in the dependent variable.[19]

The regression equations were applied to both 1970 and 1980 census data. The equation analyzing 1970 data accounted for 87 percent of the variation in rents. Seven of the variables were statistically significant. When the same model was run again to examine 1980 data, 63 percent of the variation was explained, and six of the variables were statistically significant. In both equations, seven of the variables used were consistent through time in terms of sign of coefficient and statistical significance.[20] The analysis begins with an examination of each of the variables used in the equations.

The rate of population growth has a positive relationship to both 1970 and 1980 rent levels. The relatively higher prices of newly built units, compared with existing units, surely account for part of this result, but it may also be affected by the fact that

Table 5.1

Factors Affecting Median Rents, U.S. Urbanized Areas, 1970

Variable	b	B	S.E.	F
Percentage population growth, 1960–1970	0.181^c	0.25	0.034	28.282
Percentage units 30 years and older	−0.164^b	−0.16	0.050	10.595
Percentage units with poor plumbing	0.339^a	0.14	0.136	6.236
Region: south	−9.145^c	−0.25	1.942	22.165
Median family income, 1970	0.009^c	0.57	0.001	124.560
Percentage non–white	−0.080	−0.08	0.049	2.693
Urban area population	−0.000003	−0.05	0.00000	0.775
Percentage units built after 1965	0.660^c	0.22	0.131	25.236
Percentage rental	0.354^b	0.12	0.115	9.432
Vacancy rate	0.416	0.06	0.302	1.905
(Constant)	−4.110			

R Square .88	Adjusted R Square 0.87	F 77.493	DF: 10,104

b: Unstandardized regression coefficient   B: Standardized regression coefficient
S.E.: Standard error   F: F statistic

^{a}significant at P ≤ .05
^{b}significant at P ≤ .01
^{c}significant at P ≤ .001

newcomers are less aware of housing opportunities and more susceptible therefore to paying higher rents. Some landlords may tend to charge more for equivalent units in order to protect themselves from potential "skip-outs."

The relation of older housing to rents is negative and reinforces the partial explanation given above with respect to population growth. The impact of older rental units is much stronger in the 1980 equation than in the 1970 analysis. In fact, an examination of the 1980 standardized regression coefficient reveals that the variable measuring older housing has the second strongest apparent impact on aggregate rents. Mixed results are found for the variable measuring housing without adequate plumbing. The 1970 regression equation reveals a positive influence of such housing on median rent. This relationship does not hold for 1980, however. Perhaps this may support the argument that, at the margin, prices

Table 5.2

Factors Affecting Median Rents, U.S. Urbanized Areas, 1980

Variable	b	B	S.E.	F
Percentage population growth, 1970–1980	.2851[b]	0.20	0.0977	8.52
Percentage units 30 years and older	−0.803[c]	−0.33	0.186	18.57
Percentage units with poor plumbing	2.425	0.09	1.54	2.47
Region: south	−10.00[a]	−0.15	4.66	4.61
Median family income, 1980	0.0081[c]	0.55	0.00102	68.49
Percentage non-white	−0.392[a]	−0.17	0.160	6.02
Urban area population	0.0000093	0.09	0.0000062	2.26
Percentage units built after 1975	0.388	0.09	0.258	2.27
Percentage rental	0.927[b]	0.17	0.312	8.83
Vacancy rate	0.431	0.03	0.849	0.25
(Constant)	−4.6022			

R Square 0.66   Adjusted R Square 0.63   F 25.67   DF: 10,133

b: Unstandardized regression coefficient   B: Standardized regression coefficient
S.E.: Standard error   F: F statistic

[a] significant at $P \leq .05$

[b] significant at $P \leq .01$

[c] significant at $P \leq .001$

for "decent" rental units are driven up in the face of their relative scarcity.

Rents in the South tend to be lower than elsewhere, although this phenomenon was not as pronounced in 1980 as it had been in 1970. The recent sunbelt economic and demographic boom may have helped to reduce the historical differential in rents between this region and the rest of the country.

For median family income, the outcome is statistically significant and indicates a strong positive association with rent level. For both years income has the strongest impact on rents. Income has a more widespread effect in large urban areas with populations of 50,000 or more than in nonmetropolitan urban areas with populations of under 50,000. Michael A. Stegman and Howard Sumka found, in their study of smaller nonmetropolitan cities, that a 10 percent increase in income at the mean leads to only a 1 percent increase in rents.[21] In the present analysis, the results point to a much stronger association, ranging between 4 percent and 14 percent, depending on the specification of the equation.

Median rent levels are inconsistently associated with percentage nonwhite, achieving statistical significance only in 1980, where it is found that the proportion of nonwhite persons is inversely related to median rents. This result supports no clear conclusion regarding either the degree of racial discrimination or the effects of a minority population's presence on overall market demand.

Population size is not statistically significant in either of the models. The elimination of smaller jurisdictions from the analysis may have confused this issue somewhat. In other words, when a greater range of population is taken into account, rents may tend to vary directly with population. The narrower data range used in this analysis has obscured that possibility.[22]

Surprisingly, favorable supply conditions do not appear to be related to lower rent levels. The proportion of recently constructed rental units is not significantly associated with rent levels in 1980, but is positively associated with rent levels of 1970. The percentage of rental units in the stock as a whole varies directly, not inversely, with rent levels in both years. The vacancy rate itself is not statistically significant.

For the proportion of housing stock that is rental, both equations show that as the proportion of rental housing units increase, rents tend to rise. Urban housing markets with small proportions of rental housing may not be as attractive for large profit-oriented investors. The number of units being turned over is far less than in a large rental market. This may lead to a lag in information about the value of the market and provide fewer opportunities for speculation. Furthermore, large investors might be reluctant to invest in a small rental housing market because the volume of available opportunities would be limited. Probably, small rental markets are more influenced by the less professional operators.

Results are inconsistent concerning the impact of booms in rental housing construction on rent levels. The 1970 regression equation indicates that spurts in apartment construction lead to higher rent levels, even when the population increase is held constant. But the 1980 data show no association between the two variables. The reasons why the impact of new construction changed over time can plausibly be explained by inflationary trends. During the 1960s, the cost of building new rental housing was high, relative to existing market rentals, whereas during the late 1970s, these costs were more in line with current market rents. Thus, newly constructed rentals during the earlier period might have created a ripple effect on the price level of exising rental housing, whereby owners bring the rents of their units into line with the price of new housing. Because of rapid rent inflation during the later period, on the other hand, this push factor was substantially absent. Hence, new construction had a negligible impact on aggregate rents in 1980.

One refinement in the regression analysis tested the question of whether the coefficient measuring income would be stronger in tight housing markets as opposed to loose housing markets. Inverse relationships were found in both the 1970 and 1980 regression analyses; the magnitude of the standardized regression coefficient, income, increases as the vacancy rate decreases. These findings suggest that landlords are able to peg rents to income—a measure of tenants' ability to pay—in tight housing markets. The 1970 data show that in places with vacancy rates under 9 percent, increases in incomes are accompanied by equivalent percentage increases in rent. In urban areas with vacancy rates above 9 percent, on the other hand, rents respond to income differences at less than half the rate of increase. The difference in the income coefficient between rental markets with vacancy rates of more or less than 9 percent are statistically significant ($t = 2.47$) at the .05 level.

These relationships are even stronger in 1980. In housing markets with a vacancy rate of less than 6 percent, a given percentage increase in income is associated with a percentage increase in rents that is half again as high. Where vacancy rates are 6 percent or more, incomes and rents move at the same pace. These results have important policy implications. The regression analyses indicate that vacancy rates will have an impact on rents indirectly through their influence on the share of increased income that is captured by subsequent rent increases, and that the transition from severe influence to moderate influence occurs at a higher vacancy rate than might heretofore have been presumed. Such findings do not bode well for tenants in the future if they are to count on traditional vacancy rate criteria as judicious arbitrators of market adequacy.

Conclusion

The regression analysis reveals some surprising outcomes. The predicted relationship between supply factors and rent gives only limited support to traditional housing theory. Vacancy rates have an impact on the housing market, but not at the levels that are usually taken as norms. The data show that housing markets respond to vacancy rates only at relatively high levels. Rapid rates of new construction are unlikely to cause rents to fall. Income levels have a strong positive relationship with rent—the most powerful, in fact, of all the variables studied.

What are the implications of these findings? A housing crisis cannot be determined by simply examining a city's overall vacancy rate. Rather, the vacancy rate must be placed within the context of other social and political factors that exist in a particular market. Nor can the housing planner presuppose that the market is perfectly competitive. All kinds of market imperfections are present, and they contribute to the capacity of the particular market to function or dysfunction.[23]

The focus here has been on a set of variables that are typically assumed to have strategic importance in housing market behavior. The results are ambiguous, challenging, even confusing. They confirm the importance of certain of the variables, but they also demonstrate the futility of reliance on large-scale analysis alone. Chapter 6 serves to counterbalance this one and it shows by implication that pin-pointed analyses, using a severely restricted set of variables, contain almost as many pitfalls as aggregate analyses involving free-ranging variables.

Direct Effects of Undermaintenance and Deterioration

by C. Peter Rydell & Kevin Neels

Chapter 2 concluded on a note of concern regarding the reluctance of investors to enter the rental housing industry in the face of rent control. Considering the alternatives, such reluctance would be rational in financial terms, and in the long run could threaten to make worse the very housing shortage that gave rise to controls in the first place. This chapter deals with the response of owners and managers who are already in the rental housing business at the time rent controls are introduced. As in the case of cautious investors, current owners can be expected to compensate for real or perceived financial losses. Reacting to revenue reductions by reducing maintenance expenditures, their behavior would gradually eliminate the initial price reduction benefits. Insofar as this behavior holds, rent control may be found to have transferred the social benefits associated with housing to some households in the short run, at the expense of other households in the long run. Of interest in this regard is the analytical challenge that faces anyone who chooses to investigate such an exchange of benefits.

Rent control laws differ greatly, but they have the common feature that they limit the amount by which rents can increase. As a consequence, rents of controlled dwellings are less than they would be in the absence of rent control. The difference between the market rent caused by rent control and the anticipated rent without rent control is defined as rent reduction.

Landlords who elect to stay in business can respond to the rent reduction in two ways. First, they can operate their properties the same as they would without controls. In that case, tenants will continue to receive the same "quantity of housing services" (a summary measure of the shelter and amenities provided by a dwelling). Since they pay less rent for the same quantity of housing services, the "price" of those services is reduced. Second, landlords can reduce maintenance to partially offset their revenue losses. As a result of the lowered maintenance, dwellings deteriorate, causing a drop in the quantity of housing services provided. This phenomenon is defined as quality loss due to deterioration.

In fact, both responses occur: some of the rent reduction helps tenants by reducing the price paid for housing services, and some hurts tenants by reducing the quantity of housing services they receive. The balance between those responses shifts over time, however. Initially, all of the rent reduction conferred by rent control goes into price reductions. Then, gradually, deterioration caused by undermaintenance lowers the quantity of housing services produced by a dwelling and erodes the price reduction. Ultimately, the percentage quantity reduction equals the percentage rent reduction and no price reduction remains.

This chapter traces the impact of rent control on the price and quantity of housing services. First, a model relating the output of housing services to the input of maintenance is presented. Then, the manner in which rent reductions caused by rent controls lead to undermaintenance and hence to reductions in housing services is discussed. Finally, housing deterioration estimates made in a recent analysis of the Los Angeles rent control law are reviewed.

Maintenance and Housing Condition

The key to measuring the relationship between maintenance and housing condition is recognizing that maintenance today affects housing condition tomorrow. Following the theoretical literature on the subject,[1] a simple difference equation relates the output of housing services a year from now to maintenance inputs today.

$$H(t+1) = H(t) + \alpha M(t)^\lambda - \beta H(t) \tag{1}$$

where t = time (in years) since rent control began,
  $H(t)$ = housing services produced per year,

M(t) = maintenance inputs per year,
α = constant parameter (depends on units of measure),
λ = maintenance elasticity,
β = gross deterioration rate.

The maintenance elasticity, λ, gives the percent increase in sustainable housing output per 1 percent increase in maintenance. This figure is derived by fixing the level of maintenance at M and then solving Equation 1 for the sustainable output of housing services. In other words, by requiring that H(t + 1) = H(t), the equilibrium level of housing services is found.

$$H^* = \alpha M^\lambda/\beta \tag{2}$$

where H^* = output of housing services supported by annual maintenance M.

Using the empirical estimate that λ = 0.171 (see Appendix A), it is concluded that increasing the maintenance by 1 percent increases the output of housing services supported by that maintenance by 0.171 percent.

The gross deterioration rate, β, gives the fraction of nonmaintained housing lost annually to deterioration. This figure is derived by substituting Equation 2 into Equation 1 to find how rapidly housing output approaches the sustainable level:

$$H(t + 1) - H(t) = \beta[H^* - H(t)] \tag{3}$$

Using the empirical estimate that β = 0.08 (see Appendix A), then the gap between housing services currently being produced and the housing services that can be sustained by a given maintenance level closes at the rate of 8 percent per year.

Deterioration Caused by Rent Control

In this analysis it is assumed that just before the start of rent control the quantity of housing services produced per dwelling was economically optimal, and that just enough maintenance was being done to preserve that level of production.[2] In other words, an assumption common in microeconomics is used: landlords seek to maximize profits, and hence they had adjusted maintenance inputs until the marginal dollar spent on maintenance just yielded a dollar of discounted revenues net of expenses (see Appendix B). In this analysis, the optimal output of housing services and the required input of maintenance are related by Equation 2.

Furthermore, this analysis judges that under rent control, landlords undermaintain sufficiently for the output of housing services to decline eventually to the level that controlled rents support.[3] For example, if rent control reduces rents by 10 percent, landlords realize that they are effectively selling 10 percent of their output of housing services at a zero price and will stop maintaining that portion of their output. The nonmaintained portion of their output deteriorates and eventually disappears. The final result is a dwelling producing 90 percent of the original output of housing services and renting for 90 percent of the original rent. There is then no price reduction.

Deterioration does not occur instantly, however. Consequently, during the deterioration process the percentage reduction in housing services is less than the percentage reduction in rents, and tenants receive price reductions. The size of those price reductions depends upon how rapidly deterioration occurs.

To find the pace of housing deterioration during rent control, the maintenance model of the previous section is applied. Modifying the left side of Equation 2 to reflect the level of output supported by controlled rents and the right side to include undermaintenance yields the equation defining the undermaintenance caused by rent control.

$$F(t) \, H^* = \alpha[M - U(t)]^\lambda/\beta \tag{4}$$

where $F(t)$ = controlled rent as a fraction of uncontrolled rent (that is, the percent rent reduction caused by rent control is $100 \, [1 - F(t)]$),

$U(t)$ = undermaintenance per year (that is, maintenance that would have occurred absent rent control less maintenance given rent control).

Then, by solving that equation for the level of maintenance during rent control, $M - U(t)$, and substituting the resulting expression into Equation 1 in place of $M(t)$ to find the annual housing deterioration caused by rent control, a new equation is derived:

$$H(t+1) - H(t) = -\beta[H(t) - F(t)H^*] \tag{5}$$

The difference, $H(t) - F(t)H^*$, is the gap between current housing services and those supported by controlled rents. Equation 6 shows that each year deterioration eliminates 8 percent of the gap between current housing services and those supported by controlled rents (because our estimate of β is 0.08).

Note that an explicit formula for the undermaintenance that causes the deterioration can be found by substituting Equation 2 into Equation 4 to obtain:

$$U(t) = M[1 - F(t)^{1/\lambda}] \tag{6}$$

Quantity Reductions v. Price Reductions

As mentioned at the outset, rent control initially causes only price reductions but then over time deterioration gradually reduces the quantity of housing services and erodes the bargain tenants enjoy. Using Equation 5 that argument can be quantified.

The price of housing services equals the ratio of rent charged to housing services provided:

$$P^* = \frac{R^*}{H^*} \tag{7}$$

where $P^* = $ price of housing services before rent control,

$R^* = $ rent before rent control,

$H^* = $ housing services before rent control.

That price decreases under rent control because rents decline more than housing services, that is, $F(t)$ declines more than $H(t)$ in

$$P(t) = \frac{F(t)R^*}{H(t)} \tag{8}$$

where P(t) = price of housing services during rent control,
F(t) = controlled rent as a fraction of noncontrolled rent,
H(t) = housing services produced during rent control.

Then, in solving Equations 7 and 8 to find that $F(t)H^* = H(t)$ $P(t) /P^*$, substituting that result into Equation 5, and dividing both sides of the equation by H(t), a new equation emerges:

$$\frac{H(t+1) - H(t)}{H(t)} = -\beta[\frac{P^* - P(t)}{P^*}] \tag{9}$$

The equations show that the annual relative reduction in housing services, $[H(t+1) - H(t)]/H(t)$, equals 8 percent of the remaining relative reduction in price, $[P^* - P(t)]/P(t)$, because $\beta = 0.08$. Finally, because reductions in housing services result in proportional increases in price (see Equation 8), it can be generally concluded: Each year 8 percent of the remaining relative price reductions caused by rent control is converted to relative quantity reduction caused by rent control.

For example, if rent control causes 10 percent rent reduction, then the initial result is no change in quantity and a 10 percent price reduction. However, after one year, deterioration will have caused a quantity reduction of 0.8 percent (8 percent of the 10 percent) and the price reduction will be 9.2 percent (10 percent less 0.8 percent).[4]

Interpretations

The revenue losses caused by rent control offer landlords an incentive to undermaintain their properties. In the long run, landlords allow that portion of their housing services that yields no revenue to disappear through deterioration. However, knowing that tells little about deterioration in the short or intermediate run. Rent control usually lasts for only a brief part of the life of a housing structure. If the pace at which housing deteriorates during rent control is slow enough, by the time housing starts seriously to deteriorate rent control will be gone, taking with it the incentive for landlords to undermaintain.

Hence, the key question is not whether rent control induces deterioration or by how much, but rather how rapidly it does so. This analysis estimates that deterioration occurs at a modest but meaningful pace: Each year 8 percent of the gap between the current level of housing services and the lower level supported by controlled rents is closed by deterioration.

Rent reductions cause price reductions to the extent that they are not offset by quantity reductions. Initially, all the rent reduction goes into price reductions. Then, in the long run, undermaintenance causes deterioration, eroding the price reduction and replacing it with a quantity reduction. Each year approximately 8 percent of the remaining price reductions caused by rent control is converted into relative quantity reductions.

The specific amount of deterioration caused by a rent control law depends on the size of the rent reductions generated by that law. In turn, those rent reductions depend not only on the detailed provisions of the law but also on the economic environment in which the law occurs.

Observations of rent control in Los Angeles illustrate the way that rent reductions lead to quantity reductions.[5] That analysis used the determination model discussed in this chapter (together with other models) to reach its conclusions.

Rent control began in Los Angeles during 1978. The analysis was done during 1981 when the Los Angeles city council was considering three alternatives: (1) ending rent control in 1982; (2) extending the current law; and (3) tightening the law to magnify its rent reductions. In April 1982, the city council chose the middle alternative and extended the current law with only minor modifications.

Los Angeles has a "second generation" rent control law that compensates landlords for almost all background price inflation in the economy. Consequently, the average effect on rents is small. The analysis estimated that rents were 1.2 percent lower than they would have been absent rent control in 1979, and 4.0 percent lower in 1982.

After 1982, the three alternatives differ. Ending the law in 1982 eliminates almost all rent reductions. (Deterioration during rent control that has not yet been removed by postcontrol upgrading caused the small rent reductions after 1982.) Extending the current law holds the rent reduction almost constant. Tightening the law increases the rent reduction considerably.

The right hand column of Table 6.1 reports the rent reductions estimated to result from each alternative by the years 1979, 1982, 1986 and 1990. Those rent reductions are the same for all alternatives through 1982 because the alternatives represent different choices to be made in 1982.

The quantity reductions reported in the middle column of the table were estimated from the rent reductions, using Equation 5 of the present analysis. The price reductions in the left column were estimated using Equation 8.

The consequences of rent control depend on the specific law and on the specific economic environment in which that law is imposed. The findings from the Los Angeles study cannot be applied elsewhere uncritically. The general patterns in the findings can be transferred judgmentally, however.

First, the sum of the percentage quantity and price reductions is approximately equal to the percentage rent reduction. As mentioned earlier, under rent control rent reductions either go into quantity reductions or price reductions.

Second, during rent control deterioration steadily reduces the quantity of housing services and therefore diminishes the portion of rent reductions that can benefit tenants as price reductions. For example, the Los Angeles analysis estimated that although initially almost all rent reductions go into price reductions, by 1990 two-thirds of the rent reduction caused by the current rent control law will be offset by quantity reductions, leaving only one-third of the rent reduction to benefit tenants as reduced prices.

Table 6.1

Price Reductions and Quantity Reductions Caused by
Alternative Rent Control Laws, Controlled Rental Housing,
Los Angeles, 1979–1990

| Year | Component of Rent Reduction | | |
	Price Reduction (%)	Quantity Reduction (%)	Rent Reduction (%)
	End Law[a]		
1979	1.1	.1	1.2
1982	3.2	.8	4.0
1986	0.0	.6	.6
1990	0.0	.4	.4
	Extend Current Law[b]		
1979	1.1	.1	1.2
1982	3.2	.8	4.0
1986	2.1	1.6	3.7
1990	1.3	2.2	3.5
	Tighten Law[c]		
1979	1.1	.1	1.2
1982	3.2	.8	4.0
1986	8.8	3.2	11.7
1990	12.5	6.9	18.5

Source: Rydell et al., *The Impact of Rent Control
on the Los Angeles Housing Market*, pp. 55-60.

Note: All entries are the percentage difference
between what would have prevailed absent rent control
and what occurs under rent control as of May of each
year. The entries are related by the formula $(1-p/100)$
$(1-q/100) = (1-r/100)$, where p = percentage price
reduction, q = percentage quantity reduction, and
r = percentage rent reduction.

[a]Control ended in May 1982, four years after the
start of rent control in Los Angeles.

[b]Current law (7.6 percent limit on annual rent
increases if no vacancy, but no limit on a vacancy)
extended beyond 1982.

[c]Controls revised in 1982 to impose a 5.6 percent
limit on annual rent increases if no vacancy and a
10 percent limit at a vacancy.

Appendix A. Estimating the Maintenance Elasticity and the Gross Deterioration Rate

Data from the Housing Assistance Supply Experiment,* together with a theoretical constraint, yield estimates of the parameters in the maintenance model defined earlier by Equation 1. We estimate that the maintenance elasticity, λ, is 0.171; and that the gross deterioration rate, β, is 0.08. This appendix reviews the estimation procedures and shows that the estimates have both empirical and theoretical support.

Table A.1 gives estimates of the parameter β obtained from regression analyses that assume alternative values of the parameter λ. The measures of housing services per dwelling used in the regression analysis are discussed by Kevin Neels (see note 1, this chapter).**

The second regression, which estimates β to be 0.089, has the highest explanatory power. The explanatory power is almost the same for neighboring regressions, however.

To choose between alternative plausible parameter estimates, given the regression analysis evidence, we use the following theoretical relationship between λ and β:

$$\lambda = [1 + \frac{r}{\beta}] \tag{A.1}$$

where m = optimal annual maintenance as a fraction of rent,
  r = real discount rate.

---

*The Housing Assistance Supply Experiment (HASE) was conducted by The Rand Corporation for the Department of Housing and Urban Development to test housing market responses to demand subsidies. To estimate the parameters in this paper's maintenance model we drew on a data base constructed by HASE that contains four years of panel data for 2,000 rental residential properties in two metropolitan areas.
**The regression analysis implicitly assumes that as the quantity of capital inputs deteriorate, energy and other inputs to the production of housing services shrink proportionately.

Table A.1

Alternative Estimates of Parameters in the Deterioration Model

Regression	Maintenance Elasticity (λ)	Gross Deterioration Rate (β)	Variation Explained (%)
1	.05	.092 (.007)	5.90
2	.10	.089 (.007)	5.92
3	.15	.084 (.006)	5.76
4	.20	.077 (.006)	5.47
5	.25	.069 (.006)	5.12
6	.30	.062 (.005)	4.76
7	.35	.055 (.005)	4.40
8	.40	.048 (.005)	4.07
9	.60	.029 (.004)	3.00
10	.80	.018 (.003)	2.27
11	1.00	.011 (.003)	1.75

Source: Regression analysis of Housing Assistance Supply Experiment data on changes in the quantity of housing services over time and on maintenance expenditures.

Note: The regression model is the following transformation of Equation 1:

$$[H(t + 1) - H(t)]/H(t) = \alpha M^{\lambda}/H(t) - \beta$$

It was estimated with OLS regression for alternative values of λ. Standard errors for β are given in parentheses.

Estimating that m = 0.114 and r = 0.04 makes Equation A.1 explicitly define a relationship between λ and β.*** The alternative regression runs in Table A.1 define a second relationship. We let the intersection of the two relationships (β = 0.08, λ = 0.171) determine the parameter estimates. Note that the chosen estimates are very close to the ones that maximize the explanatory power of the regression.

The theoretical relationship in Equation A.1 is a consequence of assuming that, absent rent control, housing is maintained at a level that maximizes its present value. Appendix B derives that equation.

***For the estimate that the ratio of maintenance to rent, m, is 0.114 see Rydell et al. (see note 1, this chapter). For the estimate that the real discount rate, r, is 0.04, see Neels and Rydell (again, see note 1).

Appendix B. First and Second Order Conditions for Optimal Maintenance

The theoretical relationship in Equation A.1 is a consequence of assuming that, absent rent control, housing is maintained at a level that maximizes its present value. The relationship is a transformation of the first order condition defining optimal maintenance. To complete this chapter's analyses we derive both the first and second order conditions for optimal maintenance.

The differential equation version of Equation 1, with a constant maintenance level, is:

$$H'(t) = \alpha M^\lambda - \beta H(t) \tag{B.1}$$

Solving that differential equation for the time path of housing services as a function of initial housing services and a constant maintenance level yields:

$$H(t) = [H(O) - \frac{\alpha M^\lambda}{\beta}]e^{-\beta t} + \frac{\alpha M^\lambda}{\beta} \tag{B.2}$$

The present value of future revenues less expenses is:

$$V = \int_{t=0}^{\infty} [PH(t) - M - C]c^{-rt}dt \tag{B.3}$$

where V = present value,

P = price per unit of housing services (depends on units of measure, implicitly defined as equal to 1.0 earlier in this analysis),

C = annual operating expenses besides maintenance.

Substituting Equation B.2 into Equation B.3 and integrating gives us present value as an explicit function of maintenance:

$$V = [\frac{1}{\beta + r}][PH(O) + \frac{P\alpha}{r}M^\lambda - (\frac{\beta + r}{r})M] - \frac{C}{r} \tag{B.4}$$

Setting the derivative of Equation B.4 with respect to maintenance, M, equal to zero yields the first-order condition for optimal maintenance:

$$\lambda P^\alpha M^{\lambda - 1} = \beta + r \tag{B.5}$$

Assuming that the housing stock is not only being maintained optimally but is also at its optimal level—that is, using Equation 2—enables us to transform Equation B.5 into Equation A.1. The transformation requires recognizing that m = M/PH.

Alternatively, the first order condition, Equation B.5, can be transformed into:

$$M = \left(\frac{\alpha \lambda P}{\beta + r}\right)^{\frac{1}{1 - \lambda}} \tag{B.6}$$

That result reveals that our model of optimal maintenance is consistent with the common observation that maintenance is positively correlated with housing market conditions. As the price of housing services rises, optimal maintenance increases. Specifically, Equation B.6 shows that the elasticity of maintenance with respect to the price of housing services is $1/(1 - \lambda) = 1.2$ (given our estimate that $\lambda = .171$).

Multiplying the elasticity of maintenance with respect to price, $1/(1 - \lambda)$, by the elasticity of housing services with respect to maintenance, λ, gives the elasticity of housing services with respect to price when housing services are adjusted only by varying maintenance. That elasticity can also be described as the price elasticity of supply of housing services from the existing stock. Our estimate of that elasticity, 0.2 (1.2 times 0.171), is very close to the only previous estimate in the literature, 0.3 (Ozanne & Struyk; see note 1). The agreement provides independent confirmation of this paper's empirical results.

The second order condition for optimal maintenance requires that the second derivative of Equation B.3 with respect to maintenance be less than zero. That requirement is met if and only if $0 < \lambda < 1$. Our estimate of λ, 0.17, is comfortably within this range.

Toward a Fuller Understanding of Rent Control

by Paul L. Niebanck

Rent control is a conundrum. On the surface, it appears straightforward enough: A problem (excessively high rents) is identified; a solution (public regulation) is applied. Behind the facade, however, is a set of ambiguities and contradictions that seem to defy clear analysis or reliable understanding. Just as one bit of evidence or insight is brought to bear on the subject, several others rear their heads to challenge or to qualify what at first seemed like a piece of helpful information.

The history of housing policy in the United States is full of such difficulties. Struggles to develop a federal role in housing production, to maintain a clear direction for urban renewal, to find a proper balance between income subsidies and housing subsidies, and to induce a cooperative relationship between the public and private sectors in local housing concerns have all been fraught with perceptual and analytical difficulties.

But rent control in the 1980s has peculiarities that make it especially difficult—and especially important—to understand. Rapid changes in the structure of the housing delivery system, combined with housing inflation and unprecedented household formation, have frustrated the homeownership aspirations of large numbers of middle-income persons. The withdrawal of federal subsidies, combined with the preemption of available housing opportunities by newly affluent consumers, have exacerbated the difficulties experienced by lower-income and minority households in satisfying their basic needs for security of tenure and for decent housing at affordable prices. Moreover, an increasingly mobile

population has encountered extraordinary difficulty in its attempt
to establish a meaningful relationship to a housing supply that is
provided increasingly through remote, standardized and formal
channels.

In this contemporary context, rent control has surfaced as a
popular way to put reins on the tendencies toward exploitation on
one hand and deprivation on the other that these circumstances
have permitted. Rent control has also been perceived as a threat
both to the capacity of the housing industry to serve the need for
shelter and to the time-honored autonomy and independence of
investors and owners themselves. Rent control has struck a raw
ideological nerve, created a fresh division in the consciousness of
the society, and created an occasion for major debate on the role of
housing in the political economy.

Anyone who has participated in a local rent control campaign
has directly experienced the intensity of this debate. The range of
assertions by rent control combatants is astonishing. To review
them briefly: Proponents say that it will prevent rent gouging,
protect the poor, reduce mobility, restore equity, and lead to a
more progressive government—without harm to either the housing stock or the housing provider. Opponents reply that rent control will exaggerate present inequities, discourage investment,
reduce the quantity and quality of housing, interfere with tenant-
landlord relationships, and inhibit community improvement. Proponents will declare: "The real estate speculators are robbing us
blind, and rent control will put an end to it!" Opponents will offer
the rejoinder, "If you want slums in this city, rent control will give
you just what you want!" Claims such as these are clearly over-
statements of the case and are at times full of self-righteousness.
They are neither well documented as descriptions nor accurate as
predictions. Although each statement may have some truth in it,
there seems to be no way to measure that truth. Moreover, the
arguments of either side pass each other, as proverbial ships in the
night. The debate becomes a hollow clash of extremes, and the
results are an uninformed electorate, rash policy, and a divided
community.

An informed debate must be based upon several realities: First, the housing market is itself a complex phenomenon. It consists of all manner of private interests and institutional arrangements, each of which stands to be affected by rent control in some way. Second, most current rent control laws, popularly referred to as "moderate rent control," or "rent stabilization," or "second generation rent control," are full of refinements and periodic adjustments. The clear-cut intentions of earlier laws—which were meant, temporarily, to restrain rents across the board and to divert the flow of investment away from rental housing—no longer hold. The goals, and therefore the effects, of rent control are now much more subtle, more symbolic, slower to be realized, and significantly more elusive. Third, the most commonly used methodological approaches themselves lack the necessary capacity to ferret out the information upon which sound arguments and public choices can be made. This chapter critically reviews the field of analytical possibility, suggests several potentially fruitful lines of research, and offers a conceptual framework of ideas within which rent control can be more fully understood.

Studies of Cause and Effect

Two types of inquiry have traditionally been pursued in an attempt to come to grips with the importance of rent control. One of these is predictive and conceptual. It tries to identify the conditions that give rise to local interest in rent control. The other is evaluative and descriptive. It attempts to define the major effects of rent control. Both types are intuitively appealing and professionally challenging. Furthermore, they contain the seeds of far more productive approaches. In their present form, however, these methods of analysis have virtually exhausted their analytical potential.

The Predictive Case

The case for rent control would seem to be strongest in local circumstances where the following market imperfections prevail:

1. *There exists a persistent shortage of decent rental housing.* Whether the result of insufficient housing supply or excessive consumer demand, the shortage represents more than a transitory phenomenon and is felt throughout most of the market.

2. *Rental demand cannot easily be diverted.* Peculiarities of the locality (the presence of new employment opportunities or abiding cultural affinities, for example) are so important to current and potential renters that to select an alternative area of residence would constitute a clear disadvantage.

3. *Turnover is unusually slow.* In communities whose resident populations are immobile (retired persons, for instance, or minority groups facing discrimination), the pressure of demand can manifest itself in palpable and onerous rent increases. In more transient communities, the translation of demand into price may be slower or more easily tolerated.

4. *Compensatory market adjustments or policy approaches are absent.* The jurisdiction might already have expanded to its natural limits, or conversions from owner to renter occupancy might be infeasible. More likely, the jurisdiction has either decisively limited its housing supply (as through growth management) or is fiscally or politically incapable of devising alternative strategies for satisfying rental housing demand.

5. *Renter occupants are decidedly noncompetitive*, that is, their demand position is too weak to absorb the rent increases that market conditions would bring about. Elderly and impoverished populations would be particularly vulnerable, while youthful or upwardly mobile populations would represent less of a social concern.

This list of circumstances could be extended, of course. Places where there is a demonstrated history of tenant exploitation, or where the ownership of the rental supply is dominated by investment interests exclusively, or where the housing supply is predominantly a rental supply, might be considered more in need of rent control than places where these conditions do not hold. But the basic contours are clear: rent control would seem to have objective merit in a situation where rental housing is scarce, where the renter population represents a captive market, where the turnover rate is too slow to absorb the backlog of demand, where alternative program responses are sluggish or structurally inhibited, and where the capacity of renters to pay market price increases is seriously limited.

In terms of housing markets and market imperfections, this model—or some close variant—would appear to close debate. But while the model provides intellectual perspective, in practical terms it explains very little. Jurisdictions have typically not justified their rent control statutes on these grounds. One, or perhaps two, of these criteria are sometimes used, but never the full complement. Further, rent control often emerges in localities where most of these conditions are absent, and does not receive serious consideration in most localities where they are in fact present.

Insofar as recent rent control laws have justified themselves at all on the basis of market imperfections, attention has been fixed on two statistics: the vacancy rate and the rent-to-income ratio. It is asserted that a rental vacancy rate of less than 5 percent defines a market in crisis, and that to spend more than 25 percent or 30 percent of one's income for housing constitutes an oppressive condition in need of relief. Neither of these positions can survive close scrutiny, however.

The 5 percent vacancy rate is built into virtually every current rent control law, and large amounts of money are required to determine the exact percentage of vacancies. Yet, as a holdover from the emergency rental laws of the 1940s, the 5 percent vacancy rate is entirely too rigid to be used as anything more than a convenient benchmark. Were such a figure an adequate indicator of the need for rent control most expanding housing market areas would have instituted the program by now, and most lethargic markets would have no interest in rent control.

Such a picture would make no sense, of course. In expanding areas, the speed of residential turnover and the greatly enhanced buying power that is typical of such areas are sufficient to allow renters to compete effectively for housing. That is, the vacancy rate may be low, but its precise size is not particularly relevant to the well-being of most renters. Meanwhile, no market is more in crisis than a static market in which the supply of obsolescent and low-quality housing is large, relative to the number of available vacancies, and the purchasing power of the tenant population is low, relative even to deflated rents. In such instances, the published vacancy rate signifies nothing more than the availability of inferior housing at unaffordable prices. The capacity and performance of a housing market simply cannot be captured by—and may not even be accurately reflected in—the vacancy rate alone. Whether rent control would be helpful remains moot.

The popularity of the rent-to-income ratio is even more vexing. This ratio has risen persistently in recent years and has oppressive consequences for many groups. At its root and in general, however, the phenomenon has little to do with the scarcity, or even the price, of rental housing. Rather, it is largely a manifestation of a crisis of affluence and a revolution in life-styles. Some figuring will demonstrate that, as real incomes rise, and as individual earners (partly in response to rising income) choose to live separately, their individual capacities to purchase nonhousing goods and services increase simultaneously as the proportions of their incomes devoted to housing increase. Rather than a disadvantage to be overcome, the rising rent-to-income ratio is instead the embodiment of wish-fulfillment in a population that is intent on formal independence and that is willing and able to pay the price.

Thus, the coincidence of rent control with the objective market conditions that would seem to justify it is little more than accidental; the measures of market adequacy that are employed by rent control advocates are insufficient and even misleading; and therefore market conditions account only in part for the incidence of rent control. Contrary to how many analysts would have it, rent control is clearly much more than a rationally chosen regulator used in situations that require regulating. A locality's interest in rent control has at least as much to do with underlying cultural, socioeconomic, political, and ideological factors as it has to do with market conditions. Little is known about these underlying factors.

The Evaluative Case

Paralleling the efforts made to understand the market conditions that give rise to rent control, various studies have attempted to describe the effects of rent control. Typically employing correlation and regression methods, these studies tend to isolate several dependent variables and conclude that one or two of these variables embody the principal results of the program. Not all such studies draw the same conclusions, but generally they indicate that rent control: restrains average rental increases; discourages new investment in housing; weakens incentives to maintain rental property; and retards expansion of the local tax base. While such studies have their place and a few of them have been sufficiently well designed to be informative, they fail, for the most part, to produce significant results in two major respects: First, their findings are too abstract, too remote, and too generalized to inform the specific case. Average rents may be restrained, but by how much cannot be determined without making all manner of assumptions about other relevant variables. More important, the average, which is, of course, a summary statistic, disguises the pattern of rent changes. Housing markets are collections of myriad individual exchanges, and the introduction of rent control will not engender a uniform response from each. For example, conventional research methods cannot determine whether "rent gouging" is actually reduced or whether unprecedented increases at the bottom end of the rent scale are actually encouraged.

The problem of averaging is one aspect of the larger problem of relying upon overall tendencies. Whether a rent control law is worth the commitment of public attention and money is impossible to calculate when all that is known is that the response is likely to occur in one general direction. The general direction of housing investment and maintenance, for example, may be of much less importance than its pattern and its incidence. And, in some local cases, the so-called negative effects of rent control, if more were known about them, might reveal themselves to be entirely positive. A housing stock that is marginally undermaintained, for instance, may be a housing stock that retains its capacity to serve the needs of lower-income households. Such housing may retard upward filtration and in this way remain below the threshold of massive gentrification.

The second failure of evaluative studies is related to their data base. They typically draw upon information that is collected for other, more routine, purposes, and they use only those variables on which data are commonly recorded. The time periods may not be synchronized, and the accuracy of the data may differ from variable to variable. Generally, the variables are manipulated without respect for the dynamics of their interaction or for the influences of larger forces on which the known variables are in turn dependent. These structural flaws leave analysts—and the users of their analyses—unable to separate causes from effects. An example here is the debate over rent control's influence on rates of new construction. A reduction in construction can "cause" a housing shortage, and hence lead to rent control, just as surely as rent control can frighten housing investors into taking their capital elsewhere. Correlation analysis, by definition, cannot resolve the matter.

Since the methodology limits what can be said to general statements about a very few variables, one is left with more questions than answers, including:

1. Under what circumstances does housing maintenance actually decline, and at what rate, relative to price retardation?

2. Are some types of tenants afforded more protection against rent increases than others?

3. How many landlords actually sell out, or convert to owner occupancy, in response to rent control?

4. Is the institution of rent control followed by a consolidation of rental holdings and formalization of the tenant-landlord relationship?

5. Does rent control cause nonprice competition to replace price competition in the market exchange process, and against what kinds of demand groups does this shift discriminate?

6. Is rent control followed either by collective demands for additional change, or, conversely, by a period of inertia and a feeling of security on the part of protected tenants?

In addition, most evaluative studies embody a double-edged bias. On the one hand, they tend to overstate the power of second-generation rent control. Rent control's current independent influence on large and crosscutting market factors is weak, compared with its first-generation counterpart. On the other hand, there are signs that rent control as a symbolic device and as a companion or precursor to a greater socialization of the housing system may be stronger now than was the case during the first generation. The lag in comprehension of this possibility not only reduces the relevance and utility of research findings, but inhibits us from seeing rent control as it actually is. Were the focus to change, and if more productive research methods were used, it might be possible to discover where the principal effects of rent control actually lie.

Useful Alternatives

Three lines of rent control research show promise of extending what is already known, correcting for the limitations of traditional approaches, and unearthing new and relevant data.

Housing Adaptation

Building upon the correlation and regression studies, new research would identify the primary actors—property owners and tenants—in specific relationship to each other, and it would follow their interactive behaviors through time. This approach requires the construction of a carefully stratified sample of households and housing units, exhibiting in the design an explicit concern for the range of landlord types. Essentially, this would be a study of housing adaptation that would record the actual impacts of rent control as they occur. Its purpose would be to describe the occasions for choice and change that together constitute the housing market, bearing explicitly in mind the importance of rent control on each such occasion. The study would be distinguished by its dynamic and simultaneous character, and by its interest in concreteness and specificity.

The factors to be observed would include all those that have been identified in the literature that have the power to test the current range of claims regarding rent control. Essential among these, but by no means an exhaustive list, would be: For tenants— age, income, ethnic identification, household composition, primary occupation, length of tenancy; for housing units—location, age, size, condition, rent charged, number of units in structure; for property owners—scale of holdings, location of residence, and key legal, financial, and managerial aspects of the ownership structure. Retrospective information for the period just preceding the institution of rent control, of course, would be essential, and a fully authoritative study would reach into attitudinal and aspirational characteristics as well as purely demographic or material factors.

The content—and the promise—of such an approach can best be appreciated by means of a hypothetical example. Suppose that the analytic focus is on the comparative behavior of households of different types. Further suppose that the sample design has allowed the analysis to isolate, in one cell, a cluster of young professionals, and in another cell, a cluster of college-age persons who occupy roughly the same types of units at roughly the same rentals per unit. In such a case, it would be useful to track length of occupancy as well as succession patterns, density of occupancy, and managerial responsiveness to requests for service. Insight would be gained into the differential effects of rent control on persons having different socioeconomic status.

Another comparison could yield insight into the impact of rent control on the unit and its owner. Suppose now one cluster of lower-income households occupies a set of units that are owned by longstanding residents of the jurisdiction, and a similar cluster of households occupies a similar set of units that are managed locally on behalf of an out-of-town investment group. During the rent control period, the comparative behavior in these two situations could be instructive with respect to such variables as the incidence of conversions to owner occupancy, the record of maintenance and improvement, and in general the viability of the situations as economic enterprises.

The type of study represented here would have the capacity to reveal evidence of rent control's social utility, the ability of a controlled housing inventory to render sustained service, and the comparative gains and losses to different population groups. Of particular interest to investigators of second-generation rent control would be the programs' effect (as a reinforcement or as a corrective) on societal forces such as racism, classism, and ageism. Moreover, common assertions such as the following could be tested:

1. *Rent control is a middle-class subsidy.* By limiting rents and making long-term tenancy attractive, it provides a disproportionate degree of financial and residential security to professional persons and others with job security and rising income expectations.

2. *Rent control is racially discriminatory.* Through the marginal replacement of nonprice competition for price competition within the rental supply, rent control encourages the expression of latent biases against persons of color.

3. *Rent control is oppressive with respect to older persons.* Through its various provisions regarding allowable rent increases, record-keeping, and appeals procedures, it becomes particularly burdensome for the small, typically elderly property owner, who has through the life cycle come increasingly to depend upon real estate investment income.

The necessary hypotheses, of course, could be constructed in equally strong positive terms. Community stability, it might be posited, is enhanced through rent control. By reducing economic anxiety among renters and encouraging longer-term occupancy, human relationships stand a better chance of maturing, and loyalties to the local jurisdiction are deepened. Or it could be put forward that the poorest and least influential sectors of society are saved from rampant exploitation. Relative to the abuses to which they are generally subject, the life situations of these persons conceivably would be greatly enhanced under rent control, depending in part on the diligence and creativity of the administering agency. And, it is entirely plausible that rent control rationalizes and standardizes the behavior of landlords with respect to such things as rent increases, tenant selection, and maintenance, to the benefit of all concerned. The point here is not to prejudge the results but to insist that real issues be addressed and to propose the kind of research approach that offers a means by which they can in fact be addressed.

An approximation of a housing adaptation model that would satisfy the requirements suggested above has recently been prepared for the Province of Ontario by J. R. Miron and J. B. Cullingworth.[1] Creatively piecing together a set of four surveys based upon the same sample of households, the Ontario model sought to expose the impact of rent control on the issue of housing affordability. Its objectives—to pinpoint the incidence of shelter poverty and the degree to which rent control eases its intensity—were substantially achieved. Furthermore, through a strenuous effort to apply the "knowns" from other studies in Europe and North America, the authors were able to clarify a range of relevant issues, from the rate of population mobility before and after the introduction of rent control, to the redistributive effects of rent control among landlords and tenants of various incomes. Miron and Cullingworth's effort to achieve precision with respect to these issues was largely frustrated, however, by the absence of reliable and current evidence. They were satisfied neither with the popular arguments for and against rent control nor with the conceptual and analytical tools that are available to dissect those arguments. Rent control is a "blunt tool," they conclude, but the available means for understanding its dynamics are even more blunt.

Until recently, an intimate study of housing adaptation under rent control would have been unfeasible, and the infrequency of the second-generation program would have discouraged an investment in such a study. But with the increase in popularity and longevity of rent control, the sponsorship of such an approach is now entirely reasonable. A large jurisdiction, a state perhaps, could quite easily stand ready to sponsor one or more studies, commencing at the time of program enactment. A courageous locality might commission such a study as part of its rent control legislation, or conceivably, a private foundation or public interest group could be convinced to support such an effort. The obvious difficulties in sampling, the need for a capacity to collect, retrieve, and interpret many variables, and the requirement of patience—all of which are part and parcel of the approach being suggested—would be welcomed challenges to capable and concerned research groups. In any case, the question of what rent control is really achieving in urban America cannot be unravelled in any other way.

The Praxis of Rent Control

Rent control, in its current dimensions, is a great deal more than a crisis measure or a technical device. For some jurisdictions, it is a cultural habit. For others, it is advanced as a programmatic wedge. For still others, it represents an ideological battleground. It would be inadequate and self-deceiving, therefore, to limit future research on the subject to its practical and near-term effects. Explorations must be made into its underlying strategic and ideational character.

The character of rent control is revealed dimly through an examination of the goals that have been specified in initiatives and ordinances. Further insights might be gained from a systematic study of the arguments used in public debate. But these approaches are too limited and formal. Rather, what is needed is a probing and reflective accounting of the interplay between rent control activity, on the one hand, and the political consciousness and political behavior of citizens, on the other. The focus here would be the central commitments of the rent control movement's leaders, the experiences and loyalties of their constituencies, and the perceived capacity of the movement to foster changes beyond the rent control device in its strictly limited definition.

Such an investigation, exploring the "praxis" of rent control, would be concerned with the following:

1. Whether rent control contributes to an operational definition of social class boundaries. Many rent control advocates argue that housing tenure is an important way to articulate the American social structure—and to mobilize a class-based political strategy. Rent control campaigns often evoke a rarely expressed appearance of class consciousness, and they seem to require an uncommon degree of community polarization.

2. Whether rent control brings with it a consolidation of ideological interests. The tendency to identify rent control with socialism, populism, and feminism is indicative of a fusion of purposes and a broad political agenda. Rent control has at least the potential of contributing to a different and more lasting political alignment, locally, and/or a more effective ideological network across larger regions.

3. Whether rent control is accompanied or followed by programmatic shifts and new forms of public-private relationship. As a movement toward the socialization of the housing industry, rent control would logically be accompanied by tenant organizations, limited equity cooperatives, and additional public participation in housing and development. This logic assumes that rent control is considerably more than a "middle-class subsidy," of course.

4. Whether rent control engenders a political counterforce or whether instead the shifts it helps to bring about tend toward permanency. Political opponents to rent control have several options: to adapt and try to make rent control work for them; to broaden their base and promote ways of addressing local housing concerns that do not require rent control; or to retrench and counterattack. Each of these responses has its precedents in American political life, and all of them may be represented in the political reaction to rent control.

5. Whether rent control can be expected to remain a largely temporary policy in conception and operation, or whether it will become a more permanent feature of local housing systems. Asso-

ciated with this consideration is the potential for rent control to burst the seams of the state and local jurisdictions, in which it is currently found, and to penetrate into heretofore unreceptive areas.

One study, Allan David Heskin's *Tenants and the American Dream*, has already been conducted along the lines being suggested here.[2] Focused on rent control in Los Angeles County and Santa Monica, this book offers both a conceptual framework within which to place the deeper issues and an analytical technique with which to evaluate them. With an evocative combination of empathy and frankness, his study assesses the strength and composition of the rent control movement, including its power to forestall or foment social change.

Heskin finds that rent control proponents in Santa Monica, who have produced what he calls "the strictest rent control law now in force in the United States," consist largely of upwardly mobile persons seeking increasing shares of the society's wealth.[3] Frustrated with inflated rents and unresponsive landlords, these advocates typically aspire to homeownership, and "over fifty percent of the movement-level tenants . . . expressed a desire to own rental property."[4] Therein is revealed a debate of considerable significance within the rent control movement itself: whether the movement will serve only to facilitate individual tenants' interest in property accumulation; whether the needs of working-class and minority tenants for basic residential security will be included on the movement's agenda; and whether and to what degree the progressive socialization of property will be an active ingredient in the movement's larger goals. Heskin's conclusions are cautious: "Little sign of a counter-hegemonic consciousness has emerged (from the analysis)."[5] But he offers the possibility that, under worsening economic conditions, the tenant movement may prove to have been a "sleeping giant."

In evaluating political considerations such as the ones outlined above, it is virtually impossible to conduct objective research. The nature of social movements responding to socialist and populist ideals precludes anyone except a committed and self-aware participant from speaking in more than stereotypes and banalities about their intentions or experiences. The outsider would have an especially difficult time articulating the larger meaning of rent control if it occurred in a "bourgeois" community, for example, or comprehending the appearance of contradiction if rent control resulted in harm to households to whose interests the program's apologists claim ideological loyalty. The extent of useful research here must therefore depend largely upon the readiness and the capacity of the rent control movement itself for intelligent self-criticism. Heskin has paved the way.

Societal Implications

Possibly the most important line of inquiry—one that would require a degree of critical perspective that is rare in the world of applied or policy research—would attempt to place the rent control phenomenon in its proper relationship to certain insistent trends in society. As either a lead factor or a lag factor, the practice of rent control can be viewed as one facet of an increasing bureaucratization of public life, an increasing demand for personal and group security, and an increasingly combative and litigious basis for interaction. On the other hand, it can be viewed as a precursor of greater democratization and local control, of a new and flexible partnership between government and voluntary private initiative, and of a housing delivery system that is more capable of response to human need than any we have thus far experienced.

In some ways, rent control is representative of a number of critical choices that our society is in the process of making. The patterns of ownership and management of housing are at stake, for example: Can tenants' rights be enhanced? Can they be complemented by an increased interest in cooperative ownership arrangements? Can the ideological lines between owner and renter be blurred? And can the responsibility for housing maintenance and embellishment be shared? These possibilities bear no small relationship to rent control. Will, on the other hand, the rent control movement settle for its one gain, and leave it to the landlords to make all the adjustments? Will landlords, in turn, respond defensively by consolidating their holdings, formalizing their relationships with tenants, and distancing themselves from the day-to-day requirements of upkeep and human concern? The probabilities of these occurrences seem high enough to be a warning.

The role of local government is also at stake. At the one extreme, rent control could be a step toward a stronger integration of the public and private sectors, a statement of legitimate governmental concern and of the right of citizens to be involved. It could lead the way toward a housing maintenance industry, for example, that is far less fickle and haphazard than the one we know today. It may signal a movement by government into the roles of initiator, facilitator, and flexible participant—roles that have been tried only with caution and ambivalence to the present time. But here also the negative alternative brings one up short: government as moralist, as inhibitor, as a sector that stands aloof from direct involvement and creative service.

Finally, the very nature of the housing market may be at stake. Rent control's concern for social justice and responsible stewardship could signal the maturation of this nation's long struggle to find its way through its housing problems. The goal of a decent home for every American, first enunciated at a time when household configurations were relatively stable and residential mobility was fairly slow, is today complicated enormously by an incredibly complex pattern of housing use. The rental sector is now crucial in the satisfaction of housing needs, and ways must be found to guarantee suitable housing at affordable prices to a diverse and transient household population. But, as we move toward a more universal and predictable standard for housing services, the risk is that our treatment of the rental supply will become routine, undifferentiated, unresponsive to the real differences among real people. A house must remain a home, and home implies individuality and participation, as well as standard quality at an acceptable rent.

The rent control phenomenon has emerged at a time of great uncertainty and volatility in the housing market generally. New demand groups have emerged, and the structure of housing supply is undergoing what one is tempted to call a transformation. Through all the adjustments, abiding social problems have been intensified, and certain of them now affect larger proportions of the population than has been the case since the Great Depression. The phenomenon of rent control has reemerged as a vivid and energetic feature of the changing social scene, and it may be influential in reshaping the political economy.

As the importance of rent control grows, our understanding of rent control must also grow. Proponents and opponents alike, often victims of their own enthusiasm, must not be misled as well by research that either has failed to penetrate the real issues or has rested its case on generalized findings or speculative interpolations of gross data. The point of applied research is to inform policymakers and program advocates—and to hold them to account.

The rent control field requires the application of research approaches that have an unusual capacity for close observation and critical reflection. Although the conceptual studies and descriptive work that have dominated the rent control field to date are inadequate to that task, they have nonetheless opened the way toward an accurate portrayal of rent control's social impact, an understanding of its underlying worth, and an insight into certain societal choices-in-the-making with which it has affinity.

Contributors

Paul L. Niebanck is professor of Environmental Planning at the University of California, Santa Cruz. A close observer of urban and social issues since the early 1960s, Niebanck was among the first to assess the impact of rent control in New York City, and since that time he has been involved in the so-called second generation of rent control on repeated occasions, as a consultant and as an advocate.

John I. Gilderbloom is assistant professor of Sociology at the University of Houston, University Park. He has acted frequently as a consultant on rent control and is the editor of *Rent Control: A Source Book.*

James W. Hughes is professor of Urban Planning and Policy Development in the School of Urban and Regional Policy, Rutgers University, New Brunswick. He is a co-author, with George Sternlieb, of *The Future of Rental Housing* and *America's Housing: Prospects and Problems.*

W. Dennis Keating is associate professor of Urban Studies in the College of Urban Affairs, Cleveland State University. Keating has studied the New York rent stabilization system and the administration of rent control in New Jersey. An earlier version of his contribution to the present book can be found in the monograph entitled "Rent Control in California: Responding to the Housing Crisis," published by the Institute of Government Studies at the University of California, Berkeley.

Kevin Neels is senior economist at Abt Associates, Inc., Cambridge. He has worked extensively on the relationships among prices and consumption patterns, incentives and behaviors.

C. Peter Rydell is senior social scientist at the Rand Corporation, Santa Monica. He participated in an earlier study of the New York rent control law, and he has directed a recent study of the Los Angeles law. The contribution of Rydell and Neels is drawn from that Los Angeles study and was prepared under the auspices of the Rand Corporation.

Michael A. Stegman is professor and chairman of Department of City and Regional Planning at the University of North Carolina, Chapel Hill. He served recently as Deputy Assistant Secretary for Research in the Department of Housing and Urban Development, and in 1982 he conducted a major assessment of rent regulation in New York.

George Sternlieb is professor of Urban Planning and Policy Development and director of the Center for Urban Policy Research, Rutgers University, New Brunswick. He is a co-author of *The Future of Rental Housing* and *America's Housing: Prospects and Problems*.

Notes

Chapter 1

1. Baar, "Guidelines for Drafting," p. 725. Baar estimates that about 10 percent of all privately owned rental housing is currently subject to some form of rent control.
2. Author's notes, public hearing on rent control, 16 November 1983, Town Hall, Pembroke Park, Florida.
3. Gilderbloom, *Rent Control*, p. iii.
4. Morton Schussheim, "Housing: An Overview," in *Housing—A Reader*, p. 8.
5. Cushing N. Dolbeare, "The Low-Income Housing Crisis," in Hartman, *America's Housing Crisis*, p. 34.
6. Nancy M. Saltojanes, "Inflation in Housing Costs," in *Housing—A Reader*, p. 42.
7. Emily Paradise Achtenberg and Peter Marcuse, "Toward the Decommodification of Housing: A Political Analysis and a Progressive Program," in Hartman, *America's Housing Crisis*, p. 221.
8. Michael E. Stone, "Housing and the Economic Crisis: An Analysis and Emerging Program," in Hartman, *America's Housing Crisis*, p. 114.
9. Block and Olsen, *Rent Control*.

Chapter 3

1. Niebanck, *Rent Control*, p. 20.
2. Richard G. Davies, *Housing Reform During the Truman Administration* (Columbia, Mo.: University of Missouri Press, 1966), p. 41.

3. Niebanck, *Rent Control*, p. 21.

4. Frank F. Kristof, "The Effects of Rent Control and Rent Stabilization for New York City," in Block and Olsen, *Rent Control*, p. 127.

5. Ibid., p. 130.

6. Ibid., p. 128.

7. Ibid., p. 133.

8. New York City Conciliation and Appeals Board, *Tenants' and Owners' Rights and Duties under the Rent Stabilization Law* (New York: The Board, n.d.).

9. Kristof, "Effects of Rent Control," in Block and Olsen, *Rent Control*, p. 134.

10. U.S. President's Commission, *Interim Report*, pp. 18 and 19.

11. New York City Rent Guidelines Board, *Explanatory Statement and Findings of the Rent Guidelines Board in Relation to the 1981–1982 Lease Increase Allowances for Apartments Under the Jurisdiction of the Rent Stabilization Laws* (New York: The Board, 1981), p. 2.

12. Ibid., p. 5.

13. "Explanatory Statement and Findings of the Rent Guidelines Board in Relation to 1983–84 Lease Increase Allowances for Apartments Under the Jurisdiction of the Rent Stabilization Law," *The City Record*, published by the Association of the Bar of the City of New York, 10 August 1983.

Chapter 4

1. See generally: U.S. Federal Home Loan Bank Board, *Rent Control Issue in California* (San Francisco, Cal.: U.S. Federal Home Loan Board, Special Publications Series, 1977); Levin, *Rent Control Bibliography*; Rea and Gupta, "Rent Control Controversy"; Gupta and Rea, "Second Generation Rent Control"; Lowry et al., *California's Housing*; and Kenneth Rosen, *California Housing Markets in the 1980's: Demand, Affordability, and Policies* (Cambridge, Mass.: Oelgeschlager, Gunn, and Hain, 1984), pp. 64–68.

2. California Department of Housing and Community Development, *California Statewide Housing Plan: 1980 Update of Selected Data* (Sacramento, Cal.: HCD, Division of Research and Policy Development, 1981), p. 4.

3. Ibid.

4. See California Health and Safety Code, Section 50,052.5 and Public Law No. 97–35, Section 322 for these state and federal lower-income rent-to-income standards.

5. For example, inflation in 1981 "outstripped" increased wages in Northern California. *Monthly Summary of Business Conditions in the Northern Coastal Counties* (Los Angeles: Security Pacific National Bank, February 1982): 2.

6. Rents increased annually by an average of 11.7 percent while overall inflation increased by 11.6 percent. (U.S. Bureau of Labor Statistics, *Consumer Price Index for All Items: San Francisco Index* [Washington, D.C.: GPO, 1980]). Renters' incomes are generally well below the median. In the Bay Area, renters' mean income was only two-thirds of the mean household income and only 54 percent of homeowners' income (U.S. Bureau of the Census, *1980 Census*, Tape File 3A, available through the Association of Bay Area Governments, Berkeley). According to the President's Commission on Housing, renters' median income increased by only 59 percent from 1970 to 1979, compared to a 101 percent increase in median gross rent. The commission noted that the 1977 Annual Housing Survey revealed that 57 percent of very low-income households and 22 percent of moderately low-income households paid more than 30 percent of their income for rent (U.S. President's Commission, *Report*, pp. 10–11, Tables 1.3 and 1.4).

7. California Department of Housing, *Housing Plan Update*, p. 1.

8. *California Construction Trends* (Los Angeles: Security Pacific National Bank, December 1981): Table 3, 3e; (January 1982): Table 3, 2g.

9. U.S. General Accounting Office, *Rental Housing*, p. 12.

10. A 1981 San Francisco housing study noted that a simple, no-frills, new one-bedroom apartment would rent for $995 monthly, compared to an estimated June 1980 median rent of $382 for a comparable existing unit. This creates what the report terms an "affordability gap." Citizens Housing Task Force, *Report* (San Francisco, Cal.: Office of the Mayor, 1981), pp. 8–9. This study also notes that only about 20 percent of San Francisco condominiums are priced at low and moderate income levels. Ibid., pp. 79–82.

11. For studies reflecting the view that a rental housing crisis exists, see U.S. General Accounting Office, *Rental Housing*; and Rumpf, *Outlook*. This conclusion was rejected by the President's Commission

on Housing in its *Report*, pp. 89–91. The commission relied in part on Ira S. Lowry, *Rental Housing in the 1980's: Searching for the Crisis* (Santa Monica, Cal.: Rand Corporation, 1982). Lowry reiterates this view in Lowry et al., *California's Housing*. A variation of this viewpoint is found in Thomas Hazlitt, "Rent Controls and the Housing Crisis," in Johnson, *Resolving the Housing Crisis*, pp. 277–300.

12. The Field Institute, *The California Poll* (Release No. 1030—13 June 1979). For an analysis of voting patterns in a referendum on rent control in Santa Barbara, California in June 1980, see Stephen J. DeCanio, "Rent Control Voting Patterns, Popular Views, and Group Interests," in Johnson, *Resolving the Housing Crisis*, pp. 301–18. For an analysis of the politicization of tenants in Los Angeles and Santa Monica, see Heskin, *Tenants*.

13. The cities of Davis and El Monte also had rent controls, but they are not currently in effect. These local laws vary considerably. The ordinances and administrative regulations from Berkeley, Los Angeles (city), San Francisco, San Jose, and Santa Monica are included in Myron Moskovitz et al., *Rent Control: Program Material, November/December 1982* (Berkeley, Cal.: California Continuing Education of the Bar, 1982).

14. National Multi-Housing Council, *The Spread of Rent Control* (Washington, D.C.: The Council, 31 May 1982). See also Western Mobile Home Association, *Rent Control in California* (Sacramento, Cal.: The Association, 31 January 1983).

15. Berkeley enacted an experimental commercial rent control initiative in June 1982 that applies only to one small neighborhood. Carmel and San Francisco have also debated the adoption of commercial rent control. The origin, implementation, and legality of the Berkeley initiative are discussed in W. Dennis Keating, "The Elmwood Experiment: The Use of Commercial Rent Stabilization to Preserve a Diverse Neighborhood Shopping District," *Washington University Journal of Urban and Contemporary Law* (1985, forthcoming).

16. Oakland and San Francisco adopted weaker rent arbitration regulations prior to the defeat of stricter rent control initiatives.

17. Arizona, Louisiana, and Washington have preempted local rent control.

18. Florida and New York have local option rent control.

19. Massachusetts and New Jersey take this home rule approach, al-

though Massachusetts adhered to the second alternative from 1971 to 1976.

20. For an analysis of Proposition 10, see Maureen Fitzgerald, "That Rent Initiative Scramble," *California Journal* 11 (March 1980): 1097–1108. For an account of the campaign, see Mitchell Kahn, "Proposition 10—The Landlord Relief Act," *The Nation* 230 (24 May 1980): 621–22.

21. California Government Code, Section 65,589(b) states that notwithstanding the state-imposed requirements for local housing elements: "Nothing . . . shall be construed to be a grant of authority or a repeal of an authority which may exist of a local government to impose rent controls."

22. See 24 Code of Federal Regulations, Part 403 ("Local Rent Control"). HUD has also selectively preempted local rent control that applied to federally insured housing.

23. California Health and Safety Code, Section 50,202. In 1982, the legislature authorized CHFA to establish a coinsurance program to finance the construction of multifamily housing, which would be exempt from local rent control. California Health and Safety Code, Section 51,852.5(2).

24. U.S. President's Commission, *Report*. The commission recommended federal preemption of the application of local rent controls of housing financed by a federally insured lender.

25. HUD's new Section 18 rental subsidy program can only be covered by general, preexisting rent control programs (Section 18(f) of the Housing and Urban-Rural Recovery Act of 1983, Public Law No. 98–181).

26. Rea and Gupta categorize ten communities as having either "restrictive" or "moderate" rent controls according to eight features ("Rent Control Controversy," pp. 139–40).

27. California Housing Task Force, *Major Housing Legislation for 1979: Recommendations to the Governor and Legislature* (Sacramento, Cal.: The Task Force, 1979), p. 35.

28. See Mark Forster, "Revolt of the Renters," *California Journal* 10 (October 1979): 365–67; and Derek Shearer, "How the Progressives Won in Santa Monica," *Social Policy* 12 (Winter 1982): 7–14. In June 1984, the ordinance was amended by an initiative entitled, "Tenant Ownership Rights," which expands owners' conversion rights while protecting low- and moderate-income residents. The

California Supreme Court upheld the validity of Santa Monica's conversion controls in *Santa Monica Pines, Ltd. v. Rent Control Board of Santa Monica*, 201 Cal.Rptr. 593 (1984).

29. See John Westcott, "The 'Respectable Radicals' and the Politics of Berkeley," *California Journal* 12 (April 1981): 143–44.

30. Berkeley's elected rent control board will not have jurisdiction over condominium conversion and demolitions, which are regulated by appointed boards and the city council.

31. The Oakland Tenants Union reported that Oakland's Residential Rent Arbitration Board granted 76 percent of landlords' requests for special rent increases in excess of the annual guidelines (10 percent for occupied and 12 percent for vacated units). The average annual rent increase allowed for fifty petitions was 34 percent. In 24 percent of the petitions, the proposed increase was reduced to the allowable ceiling. Oakland Tenants Union, *Tenants' Report on Rent Arbitration* (Oakland, Cal.: The Tenants Union, 1981). In 1983, the annual ceiling was reduced to 8 percent, but the ceiling on vacated units was lifted. For an analysis of the administration of rent arbitration in Oakland in comparison to Berkeley, Hayward, and San Francisco, see Jeanne Zastera, *A Study Comparing Rent Control in Oakland, California, and Three Other Bay Area Communities* (Oakland, Cal.: Office of Community Development, 1984).

32. Nina Gruen and Claude Gruen, "The Evolution of Rent Control and a Strategy for its Defeat," *Land Economics* 39 (July/August 1980): 5–10. The Gruens argue that rent control evolves in five stages, of which this is the second.

33. Anecdotal and occasional close scrutiny does exist, of course. In Berkeley, the city manager released in April 1982 a highly critical internal evaluation of the operations of the Rent Stabilization Board. The board was intended to be self-financing, through annual registration fees and fees for individual adjustment petitions. Until 1982, however, fewer than 13,000 of Berkeley's 23,000 controlled rental units had been registered by their owners. This had occurred in the face of rent withholding by tenants, enforcement litigation by the city, and denial of rent increases to nonregistered landlords. The board, therefore, had to rely on temporary city loans (totalling $261,000) and legal assistance from the Berkeley city attorney in order to function. The difficulties were abated eventually, and after the law was strengthened by initiative, the number of registered units increased to 20,220, and the board collected $724,000 in annual fees.

34. 17 Cal. 3d 129, 130 Cal.Rptr. 465 (1976). See Michael L. Maro-
    witz, "Birkenfield v. City of Berkeley: Blueprint for Rent Control in
    California," *Golden Gate University Law Review* 7 (Spring 1977):
    677–708; Hank Lerner, "The Right of Reasonable Rent Regulations:
    A Newer Economic Due Process," *University of California Law Re-
    view* 65 (March 1977): 304–19; and Stephen R. Andrade and Robert
    F. Curran, "Towards a Definable Body of Legal Requisites for Rent
    Control," *University of California, Davis Law Review* 10 (1977):
    273–308.
35. 197 Cal.Rptr. 284 (1983).
36. For a detailed analysis of the fair return issue, see Baar and Keating,
    Fair Return Standards; "Controlling Rent Control," *New Jersey Re-
    porter* 11 (October 1981): 19–25; and Baar, "Guidelines."
37. In *Gregory v. City of San Juan Capistrano*, 142 Cal.App. 3d 72,
    191 Cal.Rptr. 47 (1983), the Court of Appeal found that the city's
    mobile home rent control law did provide for a fair return on value,
    although the court invalidated the law on other grounds. In *Palos
    Verdes Shores Mobile Estates, Ltd. v. City of Los Angeles*, 142
    Cal.App. 3d 362, 190 Cal.Rptr. 866 (1983), the court rejected the
    contention that landlords are constitutionally entitled to a fair return
    on present fair value. In *Cotati Alliance for Better Housing v. City of
    Cotati*, 195 Cal.Rptr. 825 (1983), the Court of Appeal upheld a re-
    turn of investment standard. See "Rent Control Update: A Survey of
    Recent California Cases," *Housing Law Bulletin* 14 (January/ Febru-
    ary 1984): 1–9. In *Oceanside Mobile Home Park Owners' Associa-
    tion v. City of Oceanside*, 204 Cal.Rptr. 239 (1984), the Court of
    Appeal upheld the constitutionality of a maintenance of net operat-
    ing income formula.
38. *Fisher v. City of Berkeley*, 37 Cal. 3d 644 (1984). The Court also
    ruled that Berkeley's rent control law did not violate antitrust laws.
    Subsequently, the U.S. Supreme Court agreed to review this ruling.
    A decision is forthcoming in 1986.

    The issue of whether annual rent adjustment and fair return for-
    mulas must provide for an inflation allowance has been extensively
    litigated in Santa Monica. The Santa Monica Rent Control Board's
    initial formula provided for a fair return based on historical cash in-
    vestment. In March 1981, a trial judge tentatively ruled this formula
    unconstitutional because it discriminated on the basis of length of
    ownership, declaring that landlords are entitled to a fair return on
    their property's current market value. Before this decision was im-

plemented, however, the board revised the formula, adopting a net operating income (NOI) standard that guaranteed Santa Monica's landlords their pre-rent control net income (with an allowance for inflation).

39. In *Klarfield v. Berg*, 107 Cal.App. 3d 97, 165 Cal.Rptr. 685 (1980), for example, the court interpreted the Los Angeles city rent control ordinance to include retirement facilities. In *Citizens Against Rent Control/Coalition for Fair Housing v. Berkeley*, 27 Cal. 3d 810, 167 Cal.Rptr. 84, 614 P. 2d 742 (1981), a case involving an unsuccessful 1977 Berkeley rent control initiative, the state supreme court upheld the constitutionality of a Berkeley ceiling on individual campaign contributions. But this was subsequently reversed by the United States Supreme Court, which invalidated the limitations (454 U.S. 290 [1982]). While tenants have won several initiative campaigns and did defeat Proposition 10 in 1980, this spending imbalance has been a factor in the defeat of most local rent control initiatives in California. This issue is analyzed in Daniel H. Lowenstein, "Campaign Spending and Ballot Propositions: Recent Experience, Public Choice Theory, and the First Amendment," *University of California, Los Angeles Law Review* 29 (1982): 505–641. The defeat of Proposition 10, in which landlords outspent tenants by a 26–1 margin, but lost, is discussed on pp. 524–25. See also Stephen J. Burns, "Citizens Against Rent Control v. City of Berkeley: Constitutionality of Limits on Contributions in Ballot Measure Campaigns," *University of California Law Review* 69 (1981): 1001–26. The trial courts have ruled on the constitutionality and implementation of several local ordinances. For example, tenants unsuccessfully challenged the 1982 Berkeley general rent adjustment. In *Pennell v. City of San Jose*, 201 Cal.Rptr. 728 (1984), landlords successfully challenged a provision of San Jose's rent arbitration ordinance allowing hearing officers to consider hardship for low-income tenants in individual rent adjustment appeals. In *Coalition for Fair Rent v. Abdelnour*, 176 Cal.Rptr. 539 (1981), the city of San Diego's refusal to qualify a rent control initiative was ruled procedurally invalid, and the measure was placed on the ballot, whereupon the voters overwhelmingly rejected it in November 1980. In *Stein v. Santa Monica*, 107 Cal.App. 3d 97, 165 Cal.Rptr. 685 (1980), the court held that California's Environmental Quality Act does not apply to a rent control charter agreement enacted by the initiative. On

the other hand, the city of Los Angeles did prepare an environmental impact report (EIR) in considering the adoption in 1982 of a permanent rent control ordinance. This is in fact the only EIR on rent control that has been prepared in California. The California Fair Political Practices Commission (FPPC) has ruled that local officials who own four or more rental units generally may not participate in a local government's consideration of rent control legislation. On the other hand, there is no prohibition against landlords and representatives of the real estate industry being appointed to sit on the rent control boards. So far, the application of this FPPC opinion to localities has not been challenged in the courts.

40. John Gilderbloom, "Rent Control's Impact on the Quality and Quantity of the Housing Stock," in Gilderbloom, *Rent Control*, pp. 137–44.

41. Rydell, *Impact of Rent Control*, p. 7. This study also projected the probable impact on rent levels between 1982 and 1990, under several assumptions: termination of rent control, or its extension, either changed or without change.

42. Institute for Social Science Research, *Los Angeles Housing Market*, p. 44.

43. Jeffrey I. Chapman, *A Secondary Impact of Property Tax Relief—Rent Control* (Los Angeles, Cal.: The Public Policy Institute of the Center for Public Affairs, University of Southern California, 1982).

44. David Schulman, "Real Estate Valuation under Rent Control: The Case of Santa Monica," *American Real Estate and Urban Economics Journal* 9 (Spring 1981): 38–53.

45. California Public Interest Research Group (CALPIRG), *Berkeley Tenant Survey* (Berkeley, Cal.: CALPIRG, 1981).

46. Institute for Social Science Research, *Los Angeles Housing Market*, p. 34.

47. Citizens Housing Task Force, *Report*, Table 35, p. 188.

48. John J. Kirlin and Stephen B. Frates, *Impacts of Rent Control Upon the Housing Stock of Selected California Cities* (Sacramento, Cal.: Public Affairs Center, School of Public Administration, University of Southern California, 1979). The cities studied were Berkeley, Beverly Hills, Davis, El Monte, Los Angeles, and Santa Monica.

49. California Health and Safety Code, Sections 33,080.1 and 33,080.4.

50. Kenneth K. Baar and Richard LeGates, *Rental Housing under the*

Berkeley Rent Stabilization Ordinance: A Survey of Tenants and Landlords (Berkeley, Cal.: Berkeley Rent Stabilization Board, 1984).

51. California, Department of Housing, *Housing Plan Update*, p. 84.
52. David E. Dowall, *The Suburban Squeeze* (Berkeley, Cal.: The University of California Press, 1984).
53. California, Office of Planning and Research, *New Housing: Paying its Way? An Analysis of New Residential Development in Post-Proposition 13 California—Ten Case Studies* (Sacramento, Cal.: Office of Planning and Research, 1979); Dean J. Misczynski, *Housing after Proposition 13: Why Housing Construction May Stop* (Sacramento, Cal.: Office of Planning and Research, 1979). In 1982, the legislature authorized local government to finance infrastructure facilities for new residential development through special taxes and limited local fees and exactions (California Government Code, Sections 54,701 et seq.).
54. California Government Code, Sections 65,302(c) and 65,580–65,589.
55. California Government Code, Sections 65,915–65,918.
56. California Government Code, Sections 65,894 et seq.
57. California Evidence Code, Section 669.5; and California Government Code, Section 65,302.8.
58. Linda V. Bozung, "A Positive Response to Growth Control Plans: The Orange County Inclusionary Housing Program," *Pepperdine Law Review* 9 (1982): 819–51; Carolyn Burton, "California Legislature Prohibits Exclusionary Zoning, Mandates a Fair Share: Inclusionary Housing a Likely Response," *San Fernando Valley Law Review* 9 (1981): 19–46; Robert Ellickson, "The Irony of 'Inclusionary Zoning,'" *University of Southern California Law Review* 54 (1981): 1167–1216; Seymour I. Schwartz, Robert A. Johnson, and Dallas Burtraw, "Inclusionary Housing Programs: Four Case Studies," *Public Affairs Report No. 23* (June 1982): 3–11.
59. California Health and Safety Code, Sections 50,735 et seq. This fund, implemented in 1982, will result in the construction of approximately 2,000 units. California, Department of Housing and Community Development, *California Communities* (Sacramento, Cal.: HCD, 1982), p. 3. In 1981, HCD and the Governor's Office of Appropriate Technology awarded twenty-eight grants for innovative proposals to produce more affordable housing.

60. California has authorized institutional lenders to offer variable rate, adjustable rate, renegotiable rate, graduated payment, and shared appreciation mortgages.

61. This is a recommendation of both the Governor's Task Force on Affordable Housing and the Governor's Public Investment Task Force. California, Task Force on Affordable Housing, *Report to the Governor* (Beverly Hills, Cal.: The Task Force, 1981). California, Public Investment Task Force, *Interim Report* (Los Angeles, Cal.: The Task Force, 1981), pp. 6–21. In 1982, the legislature required California's public pension funds to invest at least 25 percent of their new funds in residential mortgages as long as their earnings are not reduced (California Financial Code, Sections 13,000–13,002).

62. For analyses of San Francisco's Office Housing Production Program, see Susan R. Diamond, "The San Francisco Office Housing Production Program: Social Policy Underwritten by Private Enterprise," *Harvard Environmental Law Review* 7 (1983): 449–85; Laurie Share and Susan Diamond, "San Francisco's Office Housing Production Program," *Land Use Law* 35 (October 1983): 4–10.

63. U.S. President's Commission, *Report*, pp. 17–27.

64. For an analysis of housing vouchers, see Raymond J. Struyck and Marc Bendick, Jr., eds., *Housing Vouchers for the Poor: Lessons from a National Experiment* (Washington, D.C.: The Urban Institute, 1981).

65. U.S. Department of Housing and Urban Development, Division of Policy Studies, *The Conversion of Rental Housing to Condominiums and Cooperatives: A National Study of Scope, Causes, and Impacts* (Washington, D.C.: GPO, 1980). See also Roger Illsley, "Municipal Regulation of Condominium Conversions in California," *Southern California Law Review* 53 (1979): 225–82.

66. For a general description and analysis of these regulatory policies, see Chester W. Hartman et al., *Displacement: How to Fight It* (Berkeley, Cal.: National Housing Project, 1982).

67. Janie V. Worman, "Mountain View Rental Housing Mediation—A Grass Roots Program," *Urban Law Annual* 17 (1979): 271–78. Mountain View twice rejected rent control initiatives.

68. U.S. Department of Housing and Urban Renewal, *Rental Housing*.

69. Ibid.; U.S. General Accounting Office, *Rental Housing*; and Rumpf, *Outlook*.

70. Sternlieb and Hughes, *Future of Rental Housing*.

71. For references to the numerous New York City rent control studies, see Levin, *Rent Control Bibliography*. The most recent study is Stegman, *Dynamics*. This study, based largely upon 1980 U.S. Census data, is reviewed in Chapter 3. In 1980, a New York State Temporary Commission on Rental Housing reviewed local rent, eviction, and condominium and cooperative conversion controls, but conducted no evaluation of their impacts. In 1983, the New York State Legislature transferred the administration of New York City's local rental controls back to the state.

72. For the two major statewide studies on the impact of local rent control in New Jersey, see John Gilderbloom, *The Impact of Moderate Rent Control in New Jersey* (Santa Barbara, Cal.: California Department of Housing and Community Development, 1979); Nina Gruen and Claude Gruen, *Rent Control in New Jersey: The Beginning* (San Mateo, Cal.: California Housing Council, 1977). Gilderbloom's study found no conclusive evidence that rent control had any negative impact on supply and condition of controlled rental housing or local tax base. On the other hand, the Gruens' study concluded that rent control had resulted in negative impacts, which they predicted would worsen. To date, the state of New Jersey has not studied the impact of local rent control.

Chapter 5

1. This complex matter has been dealt with, in its various parts, by many studies. Trends in rent and income are presented in U.S. General Accounting Office, *Rental Housing*. A popular account of the resultant pressure of rents on income is Peter Dreier, "Dreams and Nightmares," *The Nation* 235 (5 August 1982): 144–46. And for a presentation of the concept of shelter poverty itself, see Michael Stone, "Housing, Mortgages and the State," in Mandelker and Montgomery, *Housing in America*, pp. 144–46.

2. Glenn H. Beyer, *Housing and Society*, p. 133. This explanation has its roots in longstanding economic theory. For presentations of this theory, see Charles E. Ferguson and Maurice S. Charles, *Economic Analysis* (Homewood, Ill.: R. D. Irwin, 1974); F. G. Pennance, *Housing: A Factual Analysis* (London: Institute of Economic Affairs, Great Britain, 1969); Edgar Olsen, "A Competitive Theory of the Housing Market," in Pynoos, Schafer and Hartman, *Housing*,

pp. 228–38; James Kent, *Examining the Ventura Housing Market via Linear Regression Techniques* (Santa Barbara, Cal.: Urban Economics Program, University of California, Research Reports in Public Policy No. 16, 1979); William G. Grigsby, "Housing Markets and Public Policy," in Mandelker and Montgomery, *Housing in America*, pp. 51–55 and 226–28.

3. A vacancy rate of 5 percent is commonly perceived to represent the break-point between normal and tight rental housing markets. Monica Lett, *Rent Control: Concepts, Realities, and Mechanisms* (New Brunswick, N.J.: Center for Urban Policy Research, Rutgers University, 1976).

4. Michael Stone, "Housing," in Mandelker and Montgomery, *Housing in America*, pp. 69–81; John Atlas, *National Tenants Union Platform: Rent Control Plank Draft* (East Orange, N.J.: National Tenants Union, 1982).

5. Myron Moskovitz, Ralph E. Warner, and Charles E. Sherman, *California Tenants Handbook* (Occidental, Cal.: Nolo Press, 1972), p. 10.

6. "Figures on Vacancy Rates for City Rental Units Differ," *Los Angeles Times*, 16 March 1982, part II, pp. 1, 4.

7. Paul L. Niebanck, testimony given in *Milton Lifschitz, et al. v. City of Miami Beach, Florida, Appellee's Brief* (Kansas City: E. L. Mendenhall, 1976).

8. Baar and Keating, *Fair Return Standards*.

9. Gilderbloom, *Rent Control*, pp. 303ff.

10. Beyer, *Housing and Society*; Mandelker and Montgomery, *Housing in America*; Olsen, "Competitive Theory"; David M. Gordon, *Problems in Political Economy: An Urban Perspective* (Lexington, Mass.: Heath, 1977); and Ira S. Lowry, "Filtering and Housing Standards," *Land Economics* 36 (November 1960): 362–70.

11. U.S. President's Commission, *Interim Report*, p. 11.

12. U.S. Task Force on Housing Costs, *Final Report of the Task Force on Housing Costs* (Washington, D.C.: GPO, 1979), p. 4.

13. Urban Land Institute, Research Division, *Effects of Regulation on Housing Costs: Two Case Studies* (Washington, D.C.: Urban Land Institute, 1977); and Larry S. Bourne, *The Housing Supply and Demand Debate: Divergent Views and Policy Consequences* (Toronto: Centre for Urban and Community Studies, University of Toronto, 1977).

14. Michael Ball, "Recent Empirical Work on the Determinants of Rela-

tive Housing Prices," *Urban Studies* 10 (February 1973): 213–33.

15. Richard P. Appelbaum, *The Effects of Urban Growth: A Population Impact Analysis* (New York: Praeger, 1976); and *Size, Growth, and U.S. Cities* (New York: Praeger, 1977); Irving Hoch, "Income and City Size," *Urban Studies* 9 (October 1972): 299–328; David Russell Wheeler, "Economic Control and Urban Growth," Ph.D. diss., Massachusetts Institute of Technology, 1974.

16. Appelbaum, *Size, Growth, and U.S. Cities.*

17. For methodological approaches in which both supply and demand variables are examined simultaneously in a multiple regression model, see Appelbaum and Gilderbloom, "Supply versus Regulation"; Donald F. Vitaliano, "Public Housing and Slums: Cure or Cause," *Urban Studies* 20 (1983): 173–83; Ann Dryden Witte, "The Determination of Interurban Residential Site Price Differences: A Derived Demand Model with Empirical Testing," *Journal of Regional Science* 15 (Winter 1975): 351–63; Manuel Gottlieb, "Influences on Value in Urban Land Markets, USA, 1956–1961," *Journal of Regional Science* 6 (Summer 1965): 1–16.

18. The chosen variables and anticipated outcomes have been derived from the literature. The data, however, come from the United States Bureau of the Census. Specifically, the sources for the data are found in the following: *The 1962 County and City Data Book*, vol. 1, *Number of Inhabitants and General Social and Economic Characteristics of the 1960 Census*; *The 1963 Census of Housing*, vol. 1, *General Housing Characteristics*; *The 1970 Census of Housing*, vol. 1, *Detailed Housing Characteristics*; *The 1970 Census of Population*, vol. 1, *Number of Inhabitants and General Social and Economic Characteristics*; *The 1972 County and City Data Book*; *The 1980 Census of Population*, vol. 1, *Number of Inhabitants and General Social and Economic Characteristics*; and *The 1980 Census of Housing*, vol. 1, *Detailed Housing Characteristics*. All volumes were published in Washington, D.C., by the Government Printing Office between 1962 and 1983.

19. For the sources of the methodology, see David G. Kleinbaum and Lawrence Kupper, *Applied Regression Analysis and Other Multivariate Methods* (North Scituate, Mass.: Duxbury, 1978); and Robert F. Pindyk and Daniel F. Rubinfield, *Econometric Models and Economic Forecasts* (New York: McGraw Hill, 1976).

20. No evidence was found to suggest that possible multicollinearity problems exist in the regression equations specified. This view is

based on a careful examination of the zero order correlation coefficients indicating no strong associations among the independent variables. An additional procedure, suggested in Vitaliano, "Economic
Consequences," for testing for multicollinearity and the overall
robustness of the criterion variables, is to run alternative equations.
The use of this procedure indicates that the variables under study
were generally consistent, regardless of the specification of the
equation (see Gilderbloom, "Inter-City Rent Differentials").

21. Stegman and Sumka, *Nonmetropolitan Urban Housing.*
22. Peter Dreier, John Gilderbloom, and Richard P. Appelbaum, "Rising
Rents and Rent Control: Issues in Urban Reform," in Clavel, Forester, and Goldsmith, *Urban and Regional Planning,* pp. 154–76.
23. Richard P. Appelbaum and John Gilderbloom, "Supply-Side Economics and Rents: Are Rental Housing Markets Truly Competitive?"
in Rachet Bratt, Chester W. Hartman, and Ann Meyerson, eds.,
Critical Perspectives in Housing (Philadelphia, Pa.: Temple University Press, forthcoming).

Chapter 6

1. See especially Alan W. Evans, *The Economics of Residential Loca-
tion* (New York: St. Martin's Press, 1973); David Keifer, "Housing
Deterioration, Housing Codes, and Rent Control," *Urban Studies* 17
(February 1980): 53–62; John C. Moorhouse, "Optimal Housing
Maintenance Under Rent Control," *Southern Economics Journal* 39
(July 1972): 92–106. See also Kevin Neels, *Economics of Rental
Housing* (Santa Monica, Cal.: Rand Corporation, 1982), Appendix
A; Kevin Neels and C. Peter Rydell, *Measuring Capital's Contribution of Housing Services Production* (Santa Monica, Cal.: Rand
Corporation, 1981); and Larry Ozanne and Raymond J. Struyck,
Housing from the Existing Stock (Washington, D.C.: The Urban Institute, publication No. 221–10, 1976).
2. Alternatives to the assumptions of precontrol optimal maintenance
are possible, but implausible. One could assume that landlords
overmaintain by spending so much on maintenance that the last
maintenance dollar is not fully covered by the revenue that it gener-
ates, or one could assume that landlords undermaintain by spending
so little on maintenance that they forego opportunities to earn more
than a dollar's revenue with the last maintenance dollar. Undoubt-

edly, uncertainty about what maintenance accomplishes physically and about a particular rental market's future does lead some landlords to overmaintain their properties in a given year, while other landlords undermaintain them. However, landlords who persist year after year in running their properties in ways that reduce profits should face purchase offers that they will find attractive (given their low profits) from prospective landlords who know how to run the property optimally.

3. That judgment is based on the fact that under rent control the marginal maintenance dollar yields no revenue until the sustainable output of housing services has fallen by the same proportion as rent.

4. Actually, the price reduction after one year will be 9.3 percent because the relation between price and quantity is not strictly linear. The exact calculation divides rent, 1-0.1, by quantity, 1-0.008, to get a price, 0.907, which is 9.3 percent less than the reference of 1.000.

5. Rydell, *Impact of Rent Control*.

Chapter 7

1. Miron and Cullingworth, *Rent Control*.
2. Heskin, *Tenants*.
3. Ibid., p. xv.
4. Ibid., p. 240.
5. Ibid., p. 251.

Selected Bibliography

Appelbaum, Richard P., and Gilderbloom, John I. "Supply versus Regulation: A Case Study of U.S. Rental Housing." *Journal of Applied Behavioral Science* 19 (February 1983): 1–18.

Baar, Kenneth. "Guidelines for Drafting Rent Control Laws: Lessons of a Decade." *Rutgers Law Review* 35 (Summer 1983): 721–885.

Baar, Kenneth, and Keating, Dennis. *Fair Return Standards and Hardship Appeals Procedures: A Guide to New Jersey Rent Leveling Boards.* Berkeley: California National Housing Law Project, 1981.

Beyer, Glenn H. *Housing and Society.* New York: Macmillan, 1966.

Block, Walter, and Olsen, Edgar, eds. *Rent Control Myths and Realities.* Vancouver, B.C.: The Fraser Institute, 1981.

Clavel, Pierre; Forester, John; and Goldsmith, William, eds. *Urban and Regional Planning in an Age of Austerity.* New York: Pergamon Press, 1980.

Dreier, Peter. "The Status of Tenants in the United States." *Social Problems* 30 (December 1982): 179–98.

Gilderbloom, John I. "Moderate Rent Control: Its Impact on the Quality and Quantity of the Housing Stock." *Urban Affairs Quarterly* 17 (1982): 123–42.

————. "Social Factors Affecting Landlords in the Determination of Rent." *Urban Life* 14 (July 1985).

————. "Towards an Understanding of Inter-City Rent Differentials: A Sociological Contribution." Ph.D. diss., University of California, Santa Barbara, 1982.

Gilderbloom, John et al. *Rent Control: A Source Book.* Santa Barbara, Cal.: Foundation for National Progress, 1981.

Gupta, Dipak K., and Rea, Louis M. "Second Generation Rent Control

Ordinances: A Quantitative Comparison." *Urban Affairs Quarterly* 19 (March 1984): 395–408.

Hartman, Chester W., ed. *America's Housing Crisis*. Boston: Routledge and Kegan Paul, 1983.

Heskin, Alan David. *Tenants and the American Dream: Ideology and the Tenant Movement*. New York: Praeger, 1983.

Housing—A Reader. Prepared by the Congressional Research Service, Library of Congress. Washington, D.C.: GPO, 1983.

Institute for Social Science Research, University of California, Los Angeles. *The Los Angeles Rental Housing Market, May 1980*. Los Angeles, Cal.: The Institute, 1980.

Johnson, M. Bruce, ed. *Resolving the Housing Crisis: Government Policy, Decontrol and the Public Interest*. San Francisco, Cal.: Pacific Institute for Public Policy Research, 1982.

Levin, Marc A. *Rent Control in the United States: An Annotated Bibliography and Guide to the Literature*. Chicago: Council of Planning Bibliographies, 1981.

Los Angeles, City of. *1984 Rental Housing Study*. Los Angeles, Cal.: Community Development Department, 1985.

Lowry, Ira S.; Hillestad, Carol E.; and Sarma, Syam. *California's Housing: Adequacy, Availability, and Affordability*. Santa Monica, Cal.: Rand Corporation, 1983.

Mandelker, Daniel, and Montgomery, Roger, eds. *Housing in America: Problems and Perspectives*. Indianapolis, Ind.: Bobbs Merrill, 1973.

Miron, J. R., and Cullingworth, J. B. *Rent Control: Impacts on Income Distribution, Affordability, and Security of Tenure*. Toronto: Centre for Urban and Community Studies, University of Toronto, 1983.

Niebanck, Paul L. *Rent Control and the Rental Housing Market: New York City, 1968*. New York: New York Housing and Development Administration, 1970.

Pynoos, Jon; Schafer, Robert; and Hartman, Chester W., eds. *Housing Urban America*. Chicago: Aldine, 1973.

Rea, Louis M., and Gupta, Dipak. "The Rent Control Controversy: A Consideration of the California Experience." *Glendale Law Review* 4 (1982): 105–47.

Rumpf, William N. *The Outlook for Rental Housing: A Worsening Problem*. Washington, D.C.: The National Urban Coalition, 1981.

Rydell, C. Peter et al. *The Impact of Rent Control on the Los Angeles Housing Market*. Santa Monica, Cal.: Rand Corporation, 1981.

Stegman, Michael A. *The Dynamics of Rental Housing in New York*

City. New Brunswick, N.J.: Center for Urban Policy Research, Rutgers University, 1982.

————. *Housing in New York: The Story of a City, 1984.* New Brunswick, N.J.: Center for Urban Policy Research, Rutgers University, 1985.

Stegman, Michael A., and Sumka, Howard. *Nonmetropolitan Urban Housing: An Economic Analysis of Problems and Policies.* Cambridge, Mass.: Ballinger, 1976.

Sternlieb, George, and Hughes, James W. *The Future of Rental Housing.* New Brunswick, N.J.: Center for Urban Policy Research, Rutgers University, 1981.

U.S. Department of Housing and Urban Development. Office of Policy Development and Research. *Rental Housing: Condition and Outlook.* Washington, D.C.: GPO, 1981.

U.S. General Accounting Office. *Rental Housing: A National Problem That Needs Immediate Attention.* Washington, D.C.: GPO, 1979.

U.S. President's Commission on Housing. *Interim Report, October 30, 1981.* Washington, D.C.: GPO, 1981.

————. *Report.* Washington, D.C.: GPO, 1982.

Vitaliano, Donald F. "The Economic Consequences of Rent Control: Some Evidence from New York City." A paper presented at the November 1983 colloquium on rent control of the Lincoln Land Institute.

Index